*3

HANDBOOK

ON

H.M. AIRSHIP, RIGID No. 9

1918

The Naval & Military Press Ltd

in association with

The Imperial War Museum
Department of Printed Books

(2005)

Frontispiece.

H.M.A. R. 9 DURING HER FIRST TRIAL FLIGHT, NOVEMBER 27TH, 1916.

Attention is called to the Penalties attaching to any infraction of the Official Secrets Act.

HANDBOOK

ON

H.M. AIRSHIP, RIGID No. 9.

AIRSHIP DEPARTMENT,
ADMIRALTY,
April, 1918.

HANDBOOK ON H.M.A. RIGID No. 9.

CONTENTS OF CHAPTERS.

LIST OF PLATES.

---

o (33) AS 4751 Wt 17869—Pk 2895 250 5/18 E & S

LIST OF FIGURES.

To face p. 5.

H.M.A. R. No. 9 in Flight.

CHAPTER I.

Comparisons between H.M.A., R. No. 1 and H.M.A., R. No. 9 — General Design — Short Description of Materials used.

Comparisons between No. 1 and No. 9.

A full description in every detail of H.M.A. No. 1 is given in the Handbook on Rigid Airship No. 1. A few comparisons, however, between this ship and No. 9 may be of interest.

In No. 1 the transverse section of the ship was a 12-sided polygon. The longitudinal shape adopted is known as "Zahm" shape, that is, a parallel-sided hull with curved bow and stern portions, of which the radius of the bow is twice, and the radius of the stern nine times, the diameter of the parallel portion.

In No. 9 the transverse section is a 17-sided polygon, whilst the longitudinal shape is a modified form of "Zahm" shape, the radius of the bow, as in No. 1, being twice the diameter of the parallel portion, but the stern being only six times the same diameter, as opposed to nine.

In No. 1 the volume of gas with the bags 100 per cent. full was 663,518 cubic feet, in No. 9, 889,310 cubic feet, giving a disposable lift of 3·21 tons in the former ship and 5·1 tons in the latter.

No. 1 was propelled by means of two 8-cylinder Wolseley engines of 180-h.p. each, one housed in the foremost gondola and one in the after gondola.

The engines of No. 9 are two 6-cylinder Wolseley Maybach engines of 180-h.p. each in the foremost car, and one German Maybach engine of 250-h.p. in the after car.

General Design.

The comparatively satisfactory results obtained by means of Zeppelin and Schutte-Lanz airships on the Continent led to an order being given in June 1913 to Messrs. Vickers for the construction of an airship "to be generally in conformity with existing Zeppelin construction,"* with the following salient requirements :—

1. The ship was to attain a speed of at least 45 miles per hour for full power of the engines.

2. A minimum disposable lift of 5 tons was to be available for disposable weights.†

3. Provision was to be made for mounting a 1-pr. gun in each gondola, and two gun platforms were to be fitted on the top of the ship for mounting two Maxim guns.

4. The ship was to be capable of rising to a height of 2,000 feet during flight, and to remain there for at least 30 minutes.

---

* *See* abridged Specification in Appendix.

† Subsequent Admiralty modifications in design caused this to be reduced to 3·1 tons.

The design of H.M.A,, R. No. 9, which was to fulfil the above conditions, was prepared by Messrs. Vickers, but during construction further information led to modifications in design, which, while materially increasing the strength of the ship, unfortunately reduced the disposable lift to 3·2 tons.

The following are the main features :—

Shape of Hull.—The transverse shape is a 17-sided polygon, while the longitudinal form is a modified type of "Zahm" shape as described above. (Fig. No. 1.)

Structure of Ship.—The structure of the ship is as specified, namely, "generally in conformity with existing Zeppelin construction."*

The hull is composed of duralumin girders both in the transverse and longitudinal frames (*see* illustrations Nos. 2, 3, and 4), of a design far superior to those employed in H.M.A., R. No. 1, while the bracing of these girders is carried out by means of suitably disposed high tensile steel wires and duralumin tubes.†

The stresses set up by the gasbags pressing against the upper longitudinal girders are evenly distributed throughout the whole of these girders by connecting them together by means of cord netting.

The keel, in which the greater part of the strength of the ship lies, is a braced tubular V-shaped structure, composed of duralumin tubes, replaced by steel tubes in those portions of the ship where the bending moment is most considerable.

Gasbags.—There are 17 gasbags, each fitted between two transverse frames (*see* Figure No. 2). The original bags were composed of single-ply cotton fabric, made by the Continental Tyre Company. This fabric is proofed with rubber and subsequently lined with goldbeaters' skin to reduce the permeability.

Outer Cover.—The outer cover is composed of linen fabric, doped with cellulose acetate.

Cabins and Gondolas.—In the original design of the ship a cabin for the accommodation of the officers and crew, and also to carry the wireless installation, was provided. This was situated in the keel of the ship between Nos. 7 and 9 transverse frames. As it was found imperative to lighten the ship as much as possible, this cabin was dispensed with, only the small compartment for the wireless operators being retained.

Two gondolas are suspended from the ship, one forward and the other aft, each divided into two compartments, a navigating compartment forward and an engine room aft in each instance.

---

* *i.e.*, Zeppelin construction, 1913.

† The tubes, now known as Mallock tubes, were introduced into the original design by Professor Andrew Mallock.

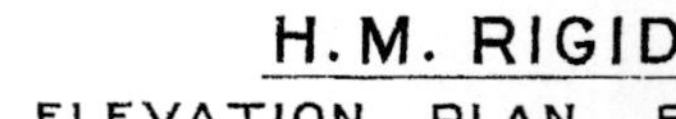

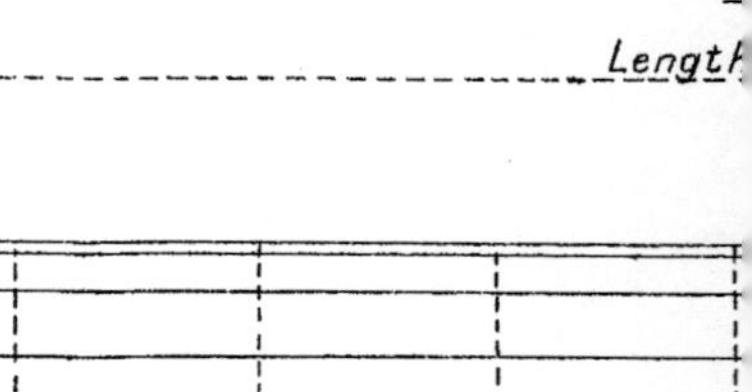

18 17 16 15 14 13 12 11 10

After Car
Auxy. Control Position
One engine 240 H.P.
Fixed propeller.

Length o

ELEVATION.

Max. Diam. of Body
53'-0"

STERN VIEW.

PARTICULARS.

Length overall 526 ft.
Extreme width 53 ft.
Extreme height 76 ft. - 6 ins.

Total lift at 95% full = 845,540
= 25·6

Armament
Three Lewis guns

Total horse-power 600
Estimated speed 45 M.P.H.

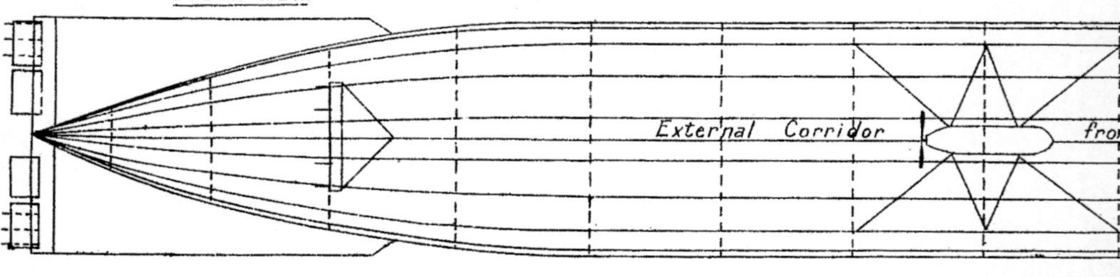

VIEW FR

7271.17863 PK 2885. 250. 5. 18.

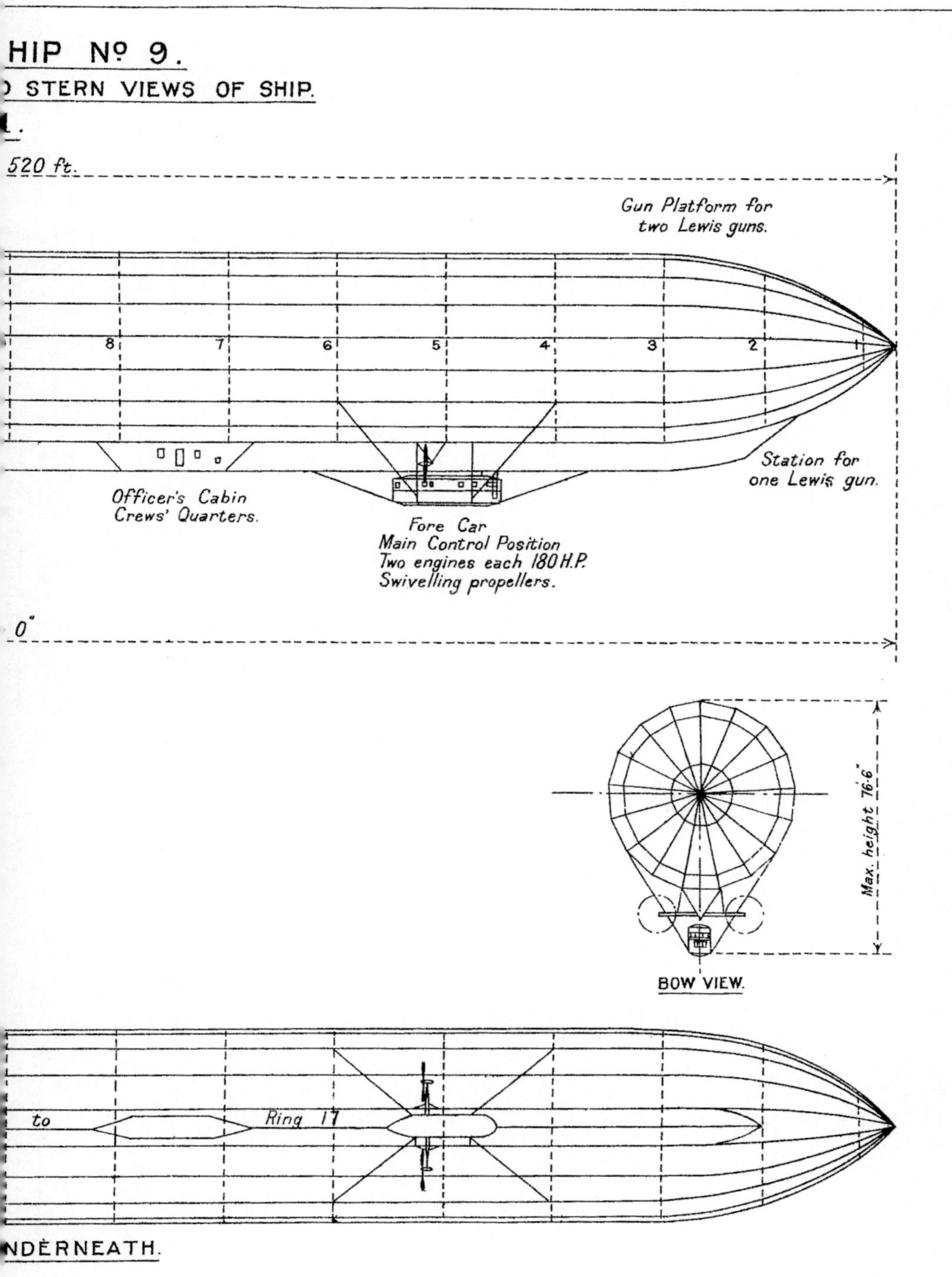

Malby & Sons, Lith.

Engines.—In the original design the ship was to be propelled by means of four 6-cylinder Wolseley Maybach engines of 180-h.p. each, two being housed in the foremost gondola and two in the after gondola. Owing to the deficiency of disposable lift observed in the ship during the lift trial of November 16th, 1916, it was decided partly to remedy this by removing the two engines from the after gondola, and substituting the 250-h.p. Maybach engine recovered from the wrecked German Zeppelin L 33.

Engine Drive.—As originally designed, the drive from the engines was to fixed propeller brackets on the sides of the hull, such a system being standard Zeppelin practice at the time the ship was designed. Subsequently, however, the design was modified to allow of swivelling propellers, which, though mechanically more complicated than the fixed propeller type, give compensating advantages for purposes of navigation which are generally considered to outweigh the increased mechanical complication.

The speed of revolution of the propellers is reduced by means of gear boxes to one half the engine speed. A further modification was made when the 250-h.p. Maybach engine was fitted in the after car, the swivelling propellers and propeller gear of the after gondola being removed and replaced by one propeller directly driven astern of the car.

Short Description of Materials used.

The whole of the hull framework other than the wires and wire fittings is of duralumin, as manufactured by Messrs. James Booth & Co., Ltd., of Birmingham.

The wires and wire fittings were made, for the most part, by Messrs. Brunton, of Musselburgh.

The keel is built up of tubes, the majority of which are duralumin, the remainder being of special steel.

Duralumin.—Much has been done in investigating and improving the properties of duralumin as a material of construction since the days of No. 1. The following chemical analyses indicate the composition :—

Analysis by the Admiralty Chemist.

Aluminium	94·09
Cu.	3·93
Manganese	·66
Mn.	·53
Si.	·49
Fe.	·30
	100·00

Analysis by the National Physical Laboratory.

Aluminium - - - - -	93·94
Cu - - - - - -	4·17
Manganese - - - - -	—
Mn - - - - - -	·56
Si - - - - - -	·62
Fe - - - - - -	·35
Zn and Ni - - - - -	·36
	100·00

Physical Properties of Duralumin.—The best properties of duralumin are not developed if it has been worked in any way unless it receives the following heat treatment :—

The metal is immersed in a molten bath of potassium and sodium nitrates, maintained at a temperature of about 500° C. After becoming uniformly heated, the metal is withdrawn and quenched in cold water. The material should be worked within one hour of quenching, as otherwise it will become too hard.

The following table illustrates the effect of time on the strength of duralumin after heat treatment, showing its increasing tensile strength with lapse of time, until about four days after the heat treatment, when it reaches a constant strength.

No.	Strip.	Sectional Area.	Breaking Load.	Tons per Sq. In.	When Tested.
			Lbs.		After Treatment.
1a	2″ × ·999″ × ·051″	·051	2,390	20·8	10 minutes.
1b	2″ × ·913″ × ·052″	·0475	2,325	22·0	60 minutes.
1c	2″ × ·999″ × ·051″	·051	3,130	27·4	18 hours.
2a	2″ × ·997″ × ·052″	·0518	3,310	28·6	65 hours.
2b	2″ × 1·00″ × ·052″	·052	3,230	27·7	89 hours.
2c	2″ × ·998″ × ·051″	·051	3,378	29·6	113 hours.

The general properties of duralumin may be summarised as follows :—

Weight - - - - -	1·623 ozs. per cubic inch (0·102 lb. per cubic inch), or 175·3 lbs. per cubic foot.
Specific gravity - - -	2·79.
Melting point - - -	650° C.
Annealing point - - -	350–380° C.
Specific heat - - - -	214 (water unity).
Thermal conductivity - -	31 (silver 100).
Co-efficient of linear expansion	·0000226.

Further details concerning materials used in the nets, gasbags, &c., will be found under their proper headings in the following chapters.

To face p. 8.

PLATE NO. 2.

DOUBLE-BRACED GIRDER.

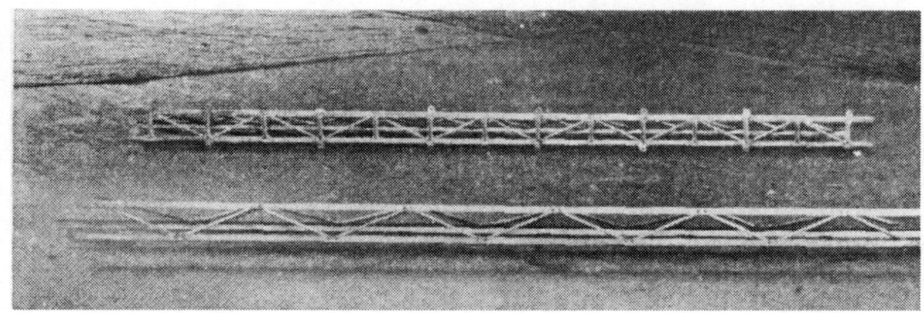

PLATE NO. 3.

SINGLE-BRACED GIRDER.

PLATE NO. 4.

DOUBLE-BRACED TRANSVERSE GIRDER.

To face p. 9.

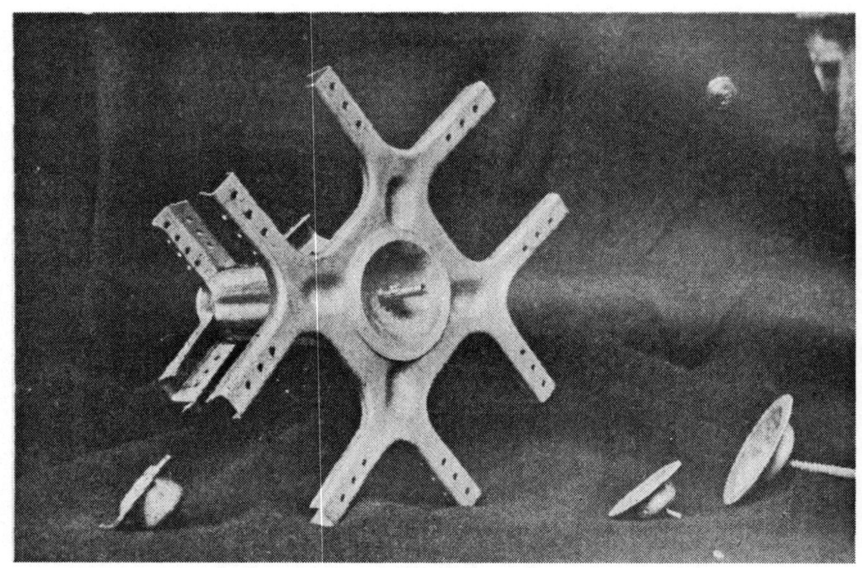

PLATE NO. 5.

JUNCTION PIECE FOR LONGITUDINAL AND TRANSVERSE GIRDERS.

PLATE NO. 6.

JUNCTION PIECE IN POSITION.

CHAPTER II.

Hull Framework—Keel and Cabin—Gondolas—Elevators, Fins, and Rudders.

Hull Framework.

The total length of the hull of H.M.A., R. No. 9 is 520 feet, of which a large proportion, namely, 330 feet, is parallel sided. The diameter of the hull is 53 feet, and the overall height from the top of the hull to the underside of the gondolas is 72 feet.

Longitudinal and transverse frames, built up of duralumin girders, form the hull. The longitudinals run the whole length of the ship and are kept apart and held together by the transverse frames, which also divide the hull into sections. All the frames are connected with suitable junction pieces, also made of duralumin, which vary in size and strength according to the position they occupy. (*See* Plates Nos. 5 and 6.)

There are 17 longitudinal frames, which, being placed at an equal distance apart, give a cross section of the hull as a uniform polygon of 17 sides. As a result of this sectional shape the two bottom frames lie in the same horizontal plane. They are specially strengthened and materially assist the keel.

The hull is divided by the transverse frames into 17 compartments, each 30 feet long and each containing a single gasbag.

On these frames are mounted the stabilising fins, rudders, and elevators, while from the two bottom frames the keel, consisting of a tubular framework, is suspended. This keel is built to withstand all vertical forces and bending moments which result from the lift given by the gasbags, and the weights of the gondolas and cabin.

The girders composing both the longitudinal and transverse frames are, with a few exceptions, triangular in section, and are formed of a duralumin channel ·9 in. × ·9 in. × ·9 in. × ·05 in. at the apex, and two angles ·9 in. × ·9 in. × ·05 in. at the base. These running members are braced together by diagonal duralumin channels. The depth of the longitudinal girders is 8 inches and the width at the base 5·2 inches. The depth of the girders of the transverse frames is 7·6 inches and the width at the base 4·8 inches. The apex angle of both sets of girders is 30°. (*See* Plates 2, 3, and 4.)

The girder work throughout is riveted with duralumin snap-headed rivets, ·2 in. diameter.

For purposes of reference the longitudinal girders are lettered from A to J, port and starboard, A being the walking-way girder at the top of the hull and girders JJ being the girders which carry the keel. The following are details of the longitudinal girders :—

Girder A, the walking way, is a special box girder, the top covered with a corrugated duralumin plate. The weight of this is 1·25 lbs. per foot run.

Girders B and C are partially double-braced, that is, double-braced at each end and at the centre, the remaining portion being single-braced.

Girders D, E, and F are entirely single-braced.

Girders G and H are partially double-braced.

Girders J are double-braced throughout.

At the nose of the ship the girder work is carried to the extreme end and connected to a duralumin nosecap. The tail of the ship is made up of duralumin channels, which converge to a point and are riveted to a cone. (*See* Plates Nos. 7, 8, and 9.)

The general arrangement of girders throughout the transverse frames is similar in design. From girder A to girder G the girders are single-braced. From girder G to girder J the girders are double-braced, the weight of these girders being ·66 lb. per foot run.

The girders connecting the JJ girders are single-braced except where the cabin occurs, when they are double-braced.

A special girder carries the petrol and water ballast tanks and takes the place of the girder connecting the JJ girders. This is a single-braced box girder, with four duralumin straps passing over the top of the tank and secured with bolts.

It has been found by experience that the girders in the transverse frames between A and B, and B and C are liable to buckle when the bags are under pressure. This actually occurred at transverse frame No. 3 when tests of the gas valves were being carried out, as will be seen in a later chapter.

In the No. 23 class these upper girders of the transverse frames are double-braced, and spare girders of the same construction were supplied for No. 9.

Intermediately between each pair of main transverse frames are two light rings of tubes completely encircling the section.

These tubes, known as Mallock tubes, give an additional support to the longitudinal members of the hull, which are themselves connected together by means of nets, while the rectangles made by adjacent longitudinal girders, Mallock tubes, and main transverse frames are diagonally braced by means of steel wires. The weight of these tubes per foot run is ·216 lb., their strength as a strut being 600 lbs. direct load.

The transverse system is also braced by means of wires, these wires forming two distinct systems, one termed radial wiring and the other lift wiring.

The general functions of the various components of a section of hull may be described as follows :—

Radial Wiring of Transverse Frame.—This wiring performs functions similar to those of the spokes of a bicycle wheel; it enables the transverse frame to maintain its shape.

To tighten up the wires to take the correct stresses, they meet at the centre at a steel ring, through which they are threaded and secured by nuts. To prevent chafing of the gasbags these rings are covered by a two-ply fabric patch.

H.M.

ARRANGEME

Fi

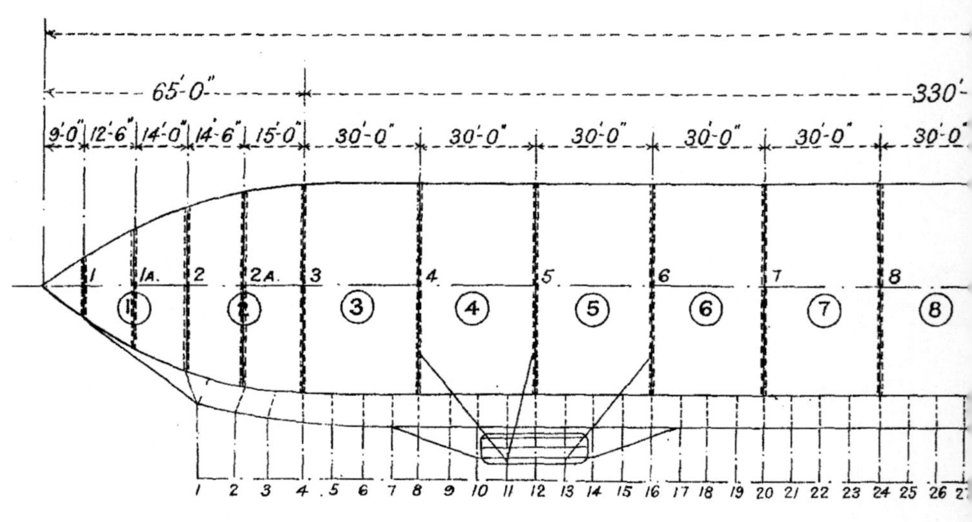

EL

Nº OF FRAME.	DIAMETER OVER CORNERS	LENGTH OF SIDE CORNER TO CORNER
1	15' - 3".99	2' - 9".81
1A.	31' - 3".41	5' - 8".98
2	43' - 3".94	7' - 11".54
2A.	50' - 6".29	9' - 3".408
3 - 14	53' - 0"	9' - 8".87
15	50' - 0".55	9' - 2".35
16	41' - 10".01	7' - 8".24
17	29' - 1".87	5' - 4".29
17A.	21' - 4".85	3' - 11".19
18	14' - 2".15	2' - 7".27

Nº 9.

F SHIP.

2.

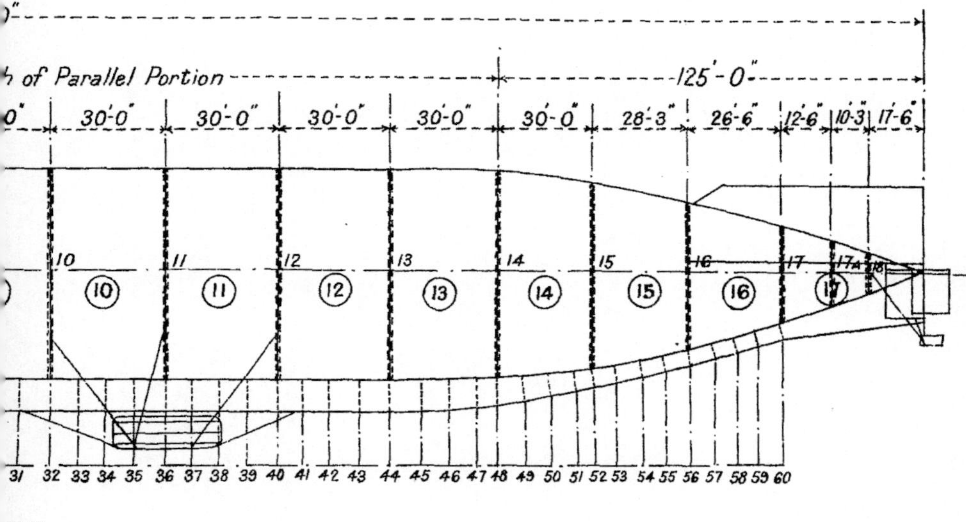

ON.

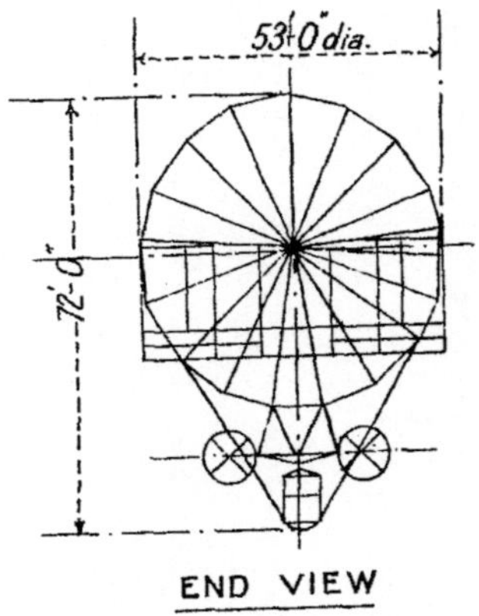

END VIEW

Malby & Sons, Lith.

To face p. 10.

PLATE NO. 7.
FRAMEWORK OF BOW PORTION OF SHIP.

To face p. 11.

Plate No. 8.

Hull Framework looking towards Stern.

To face p. 11.

PLATE No. 9.

HULL FRAMEWORK. FRAMES 17, 17A, AND 18, TOWARDS STERN.

Lift Wires.—These wires, it will be seen, come to the two points on the transverse frame which are attached to the keel. When the gasbag is inflated, the bag itself presses upon the longitudinal girders at the top of the ship; this pressure is transferred to the transverse frame, and thence by means of the various lift wires to the keel. Thus, the stresses set up by the gas are ultimately brought to the keel, which, as has already been said, is the main strength of the whole ship.

The accompanying table gives some details of the wiring of a standard transverse frame.

Details of Wiring in Standard Transverse Frame—Parallel Portion.

Purpose.	Length Overall.	Diameter of Wire.	Number required for one Frame.
		mm.	
Joint centre wires - - -	7·1″	4·5	14
Joint centre wires, joints A and J -	7·1″	6·0	3
Radial wires - - - -	25′ 8·75″	3·0	17
Suspension wires, joint A - -	50′ 3″	3·0	2
Suspension wires, joint B - -	49′ 3″	3·5	2
Suspension wires, joint C - -	46′ 3″	3·5	2
Suspension wires, joint D - -	40′ 3″	3·5	2
Suspension wires, joint E - -	33′ 9″	3·5	2
Suspension wires, joint F - -	26′ 0″	3·5	2
Suspension wires, joint G - -	17′ 9″	3·5	2
Junction wires, joint A - - -	1′ 3·72″	3·0	2
Junction wires, joint B - - -	1′ 1·3″	3·5	2
Junction wires, joint C - -	6·2″	3·5	2
Junction wires, joint D - -	1′ 4·07″	3·5	2
Junction wires, joint E - - -	1′ 2·77″	3·5	2
Junction wires, joint F - -	1′ 2·04″	3·5	2
Junction wires, joint G - - -	8·1″	3·5	2

Of the above wires, the following are butted and screwed at both ends :—

(1) Joint centre wires.
(2) Radial wires.
(3) Suspension junction wires.
(4) Suspension wires at joint "A."

The following are fitted with standard butted head at one end and butted and screwed at the other :—

(1) Suspension wires other than at joint "A."

Nets.

The nets, which connect adjacent longitudinal frames, distribute the pressure on the upper longitudinal frames evenly throughout the whole series. Besides performing this function, the nets also prevent the gasbags from chafing on the diagonal wiring or pressing their way at the top of the ship right up to the outer cover. These last two functions of the nets are useful but the equalising of the longitudinal frame stresses is the most important duty that they carry out. They are attached to lugs on the base of the longitudinal girders. These lugs are a continuation of the distance pieces on either edge of the base of the girders and are spaced 1 ft. $5\frac{3}{4}$ in. centres. The tautening of the nets is effected by strings which attach the nets to the lugs and can be regulated as required.

The tension varies between nil from longitudinal girders A to B to 54 lbs. between the JJ girders.

The fabric covering strips to the bases of the longitudinal girders, as described in the next chapter, are also attached to the same lugs on the girders.

These nets are made of No. 6 kite cord, proofed. The strength of the strands is ·336 lb. per string.

Strength of the nets as manufactured, 150 lbs. per foot run.

Weight of the cord, 29 ozs. per 100 yards.

Total weight in the ship, ·439 ton.

Keel.

The keel is triangular in section and is composed chiefly of duralumin tubes with steel ball ends fitting into drop forged steel junction pieces, the whole structure depending for its rigidity on its bracing wires. (Plate No. 10.)

At those points in the keel where the bending moment of the whole ship is most considerable, steel tubes replace horizontal duralumin ones at the apex of the triangle of the keel.

In addition to its other functions the keel acts as a walking-way to connect up the gondolas and the cabin.

The walking-way is formed by a single-braced girder, triangular in section, fitting in the apex of the keel. The base of this girder, which forms the walking-way, is covered with a corrugated duralumin plating.

The keel is widened out to take the cabin, where it forms a trapezium in section. A single-braced girder is here introduced at floor level to give additional strength. (*See* Plate No. 11.)

The following are the sizes and weights of the longitudinal keel tubes :—

Top Longitudinals.

Diameter.	Thick.	Weight per Foot.
2·44 in.	·07 in.	·66 lb.
2·5 in.	·10 in.	·933 lb.
3·4 in.	·10 in.	1·28 lbs.
3·5 in.	·15 in.	1·95 lbs.
2·6 in.	·15 in.	1·43 lbs.

To face p. 12.

PLATE No. 10.

KEEL MEMBERS.

To face p. 13.

PLATE No. 11.

STEEL MEMBERS IN WAY OF CABIN.

Bottom Longitudinals.

Diameter.	Thick.	Weight per Foot.
3·4 in.	·10 in.	1·28 lbs.
3·5 in.	·15 in.	1·95 lbs.
3·5 in.	·20 in.	2·57 lbs.
4·0 in.	15 G	3·15 lbs. (steel)
4·0 in.	12 G	4·57 lbs. (steel)
4·0 in.	11 G	5·11 lbs. (steel)
4·0 in.	10 G	6·38 lbs. (steel)

Strength and Weight of Vertical Duralumin Tubes.

Diameter.	Thickness.	Weight.	Strength in Compression.
In.	In.	Lbs.	Lbs.
2·26	·08	·77	2,200
2·30	·01	·97	3,200
2·46	·18	1·82	6,000
2·35	·125	1·24	4,000

Strength of Keel Bracing Wires.

Diameter.	Ultimate Strength.
4 mm.	1·25 tons.
6 mm.	2·80 tons.
8 mm.	5·00 tons.

Top Walking-Way.

The top walking-way of the ship extends from frame No. 2 to frame No. 16. The longitudinal girder which carries this is specially strengthened as before mentioned, and covered with a corrugated duralumin plate.

A canvas fabric cover is stuck over the outer cover to prevent wear A life line is carried throughout the length of the walking-way, passing through eyebolts attached to each transverse frame. This life line is extended along the upper vertical fin to afford a safeguard in the event of gas valves or elevators requiring attention.

Climbing Tube.

This is situated just aft of No. 3 transverse frame, the centre line of the tube being 2 ft. 7 in. aft of the centre line of the transverse frame. It is composed of duralumin channels braced together, giving a section of a regular hexagon, and is formed of eight detachable sections.

The gun platform itself is composed of duralumin sections, and is in plan a regular polygon of 12 sides, 4 ft. 6 in. across the corners, covered by a corrugated plate ·03 inch thick. A door, hinged to lift upwards, can be closed when the platform is not in use. (*See* Plate No. 37.)

Method of Erection and Slinging the Ship.

The ship was erected and supported on cradles consisting of steel angles bent to the necessary radius, on which the ship could revolve by means of rollers fixed on the outsides of the corner joints. These rollers in their lowest position were about 3 feet off the ground and, to enable the keel and cars to be fitted, it was necessary to lift the ship off the cradles and support her about 18 feet higher. This was accomplished in the following manner on 28th and 29th June 1916.

Slings were arranged under the ship, consisting of two parts of 1¼-inch F.S. wire at each transverse frame, one part coming each side of the cradle rollers, lightly stopped to the frame to prevent them spreading.

In order to prevent excessive strain being brought on any particular transverse frame due to unequal lifting, a runner was led from each end of the sling through a single block and down to a wooden tray loaded with weights. To these single blocks purchases were attached from wire slings coming from the roof, and the hauling parts of the purchases were brought down to the floor of the shed. (*See* Fig. No. 3.)

There were 18 purchases at each side at frames 1 to 18 inclusive.

The weights on the trays at the respective frames were as follows :—

	Lbs.
Frame 1, weight each side - - -	293
„ 2, „ „ - - -	426
„ 3, „ „ - - -	515
„ 4, „ „ - - -	476
„ 5, „ „ - - -	522
„ 6, „ „ - - -	539
„ 7, „ „ - - -	457
„ 8, „ „ - - -	449
„ 9, „ „ - - -	454
„ 10, „ „ - - -	477
„ 11, „ „ - - -	521
„ 12, „ „ - - -	481
„ 13, „ „ - - -	454
„ 14, „ „ - - -	453
„ 15, „ „ - - -	435
„ 16, „ „ - - -	466
„ 17, „ „ - - -	425
„ 18, „ „ - - -	247

DIAGRAM SHOWING METHOD OF SLINGING THE SHIP.

Fig. Nº 3.

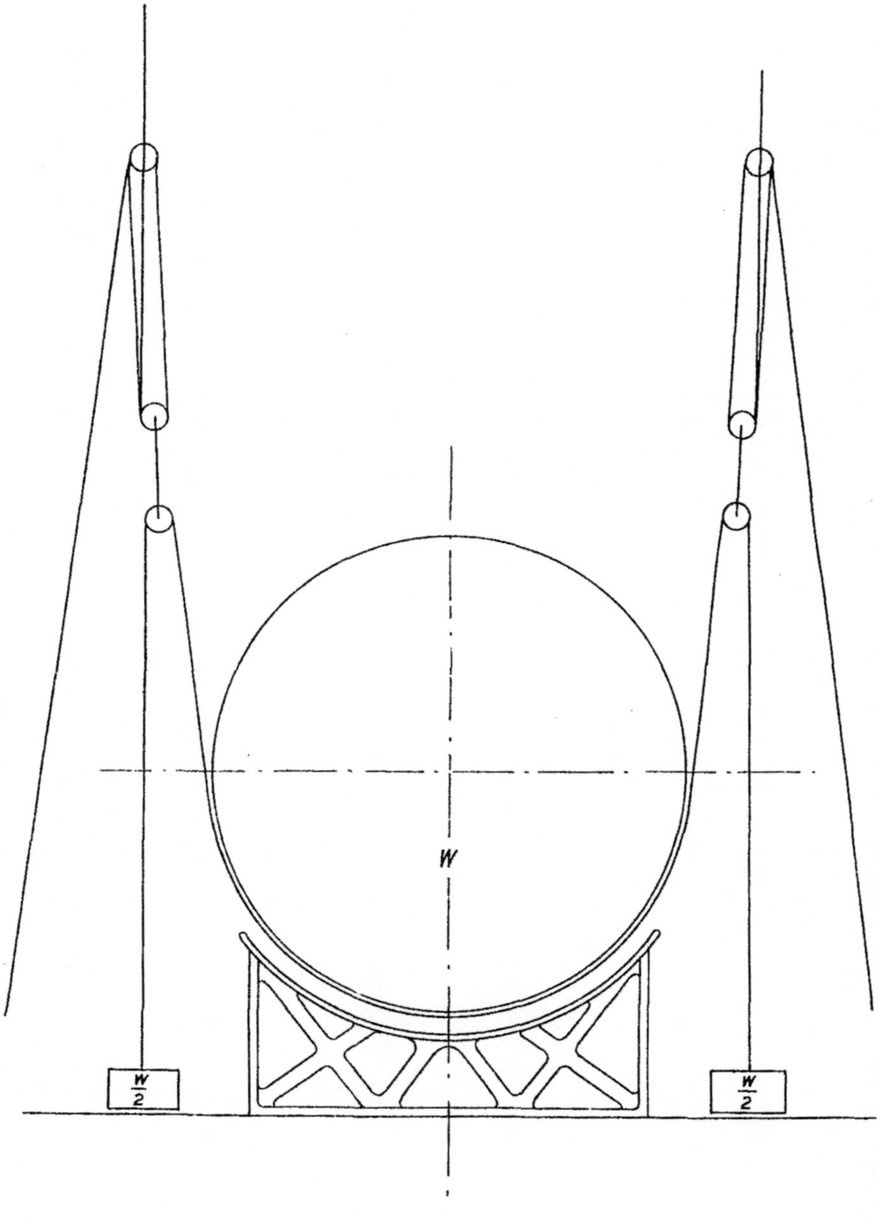

W

W/2

W/2

7271.

Mallby & Sons, Lith.

To face p. 14.

PLATE NO. 12.
SHOWING HULL SLUNG.

To face p 15.

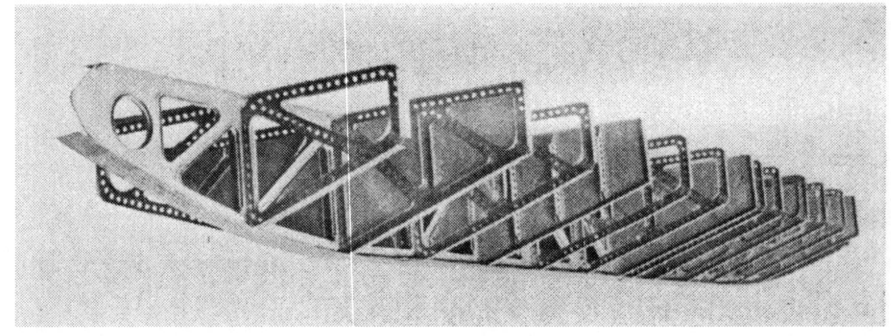

PLATE No. 13.

FLOOR GIRDERS OF GONDOLA.

The effect of this arrangement was intended to be that if to any purchase too much effort was applied by the men hoisting the ship, the counterpoise weight would merely be raised from the shed floor, thus giving warning to the men on the purchase, and automatically preventing more than a lift equivalent to approximately the weight on the tray being applied to the frame.

The hoisting tackle provided by Messrs. Vickers was rather lighter than is considered advisable, both from a strength and handling point of view.

The purchases consisted of a three-fold block and a two-fold block, with 1½-in. white hemp rope.

The lifting was carried out entirely by Messrs. Vickers' officials and men. At the first attempt to lift the ship, the hook of the upper block of No. 13 tackle port became unhooked owing to bad "mousing," and later a similar mishap took place at No. 3 tackle starboard.

Owing to friction of the rope runners through the single blocks, the weights first put on the trays proved scarcely sufficient, especially for the after part of the ship, since the ship appeared to lift easier forward than aft.

It was also noticed that the ship lifted slightly more the starboard side than the port side, *i.e.*, with a slight list to port, and that, owing to the points of attachment of the purchases to the roof, she did not lift quite vertically off the cradles, but tended to take up a position slightly to starboard of the fore and aft centre line.

This caused the after part of the ship to come dangerously near, and in fact just touch some scaffolding which had been erected for trying on the horizontal fin. It was necessary to use a temporary guy to keep the ship off this scaffolding.

The ship was lifted about 2 feet from the cradles and secured in this position for the night.

It is considered that the system on the whole fulfilled the purpose for which it was designed, but that it would have been better had the runners been of wire.

The fact that on two occasions a frame was left entirely unsupported owing to breakage of purchase parts, without apparent damage, and the general behaviour of the hull under the handling received, gave the impression that the hull was quite strong and well built.

It seems at least doubtful whether the complication of the counterpoise weight system is really necessary, if properly instructed men are available for the work, although it was of value under the circumstances in which No. 9 was lifted.

On the next day the lifting was completed without further incident, the ship being raised through a total height of 18 feet. (Plate No. 12.)

Gondolas.

The ship is provided with two gondolas, slung fore and aft, each designed to carry the navigating personnel and the necessary instruments, &c., and also the power units for the propulsion of the ship. These gondolas are each 30 feet long, 6 feet wide, and 8 ft. 9 ins. deep overall. The undersides of both gondolas were originally 10 ft. 6 ins. below the keel of the ship, but the after gondola was dropped a further 12 ins. when the alterations to the machinery were effected, in order to accommodate the single large propeller at the stern of the car.

The centre of the forward gondola is slung directly beneath No. 5 transverse frame, and the centre of the after gondola beneath No. 11 frame.

The design of these gondolas was calculated with a view to offering the least amount of head resistance to the wind.

The leading features of the construction are as follows :—

One main girder, formed of duralumin sections, runs the full length along the centre line of the car. The top flange of this girder is the floor level, the depth being 2 ft. practically throughout, each end being slightly tapered. 32 transverse girders, spaced at slightly irregular intervals, support the main loads carried in the car. These act as cantilevers, and are connected to the web of the main girder. (Plate No. 13.) Vertical standards to carry the outside sheeting, with a connecting member to support the roof covering and stiffen up the whole superstructure, are carried by the transverse girders. The whole exterior of the car is covered with a sheeting of duralumin plates, the floor itself being composed of similar material.

The cars are suspended in the following manner. Two steel tubes, fitting into a steel junction piece at each end, are bolted to brackets at floor level at each end of the transverse girders. These meet at an apex just above roof level and are carried by the Mallock tubes forming the keel at the next bay each side of the centre line of the car. In addition to these, two steel wire suspensions support the weight at each connection of the steel tube to the bracket before mentioned, the forward suspensions running from transverse frames Nos. 4 and 5 and the after from frames 5 and 6. The suspension is completed by a steel wire running from the keel of the ship both to the fore and after ends of the car.

The design, in the main, is identical in both gondolas, though different arrangements of engine bearers are required to carry the different power units of each car.

The engine room is divided from the navigation compartment by means of a bulkhead, a door being provided for communication.

The car is fitted with windows, two in each car of ordinary glass, the remainder of cellon, and is entered by a doorway in the side.

The controls and instruments will be dealt with in their appropriate chapters.

The service petrol tank is carried in the engine room.

To face p. 16.

PLATE No. 14.

AFTER GONDOLA SHOWING ALTERATIONS WITH SINGLE ENGINE FITTED.

To face p. 17.

PLATE No. 15.

WIRELESS CABIN.

Access to the keel walking-way is provided by means of a ladder.

In the forward car only, a chart table with an extension flap is provided. The framework is composed of duralumin sections, the top being made of three-ply wood, the total weight being about 10½ lbs.

A handling rail is fitted on both sides of each gondola for the convenience of the landing party in handling the ship. (Plate No. 14.)

The gondolas were originally fitted with two swivelling landing wheels each, with buffer gear to absorb shock. Continual trouble was experienced with them, and, after the arrival of the ship at Howden, they were removed and a Palmer cord bumping bag was fitted to each car.

In the deck of the forward part of the gondola two observation trunks were fitted.

Buoyancy bags were fitted beneath the decking of the cars. These bags were made in pairs to lie each side of the main keel and were connected together. In each car there are eight pairs of these bags, the total capacity being 144 cubic feet per car. A fabric cover is solutioned to the inside of the bottom plating to render the whole water-tight.

W.T. Cabin.

A small compartment in the keel of the ship is fitted as a W/T cabin. This occurs between frames Nos. 26 and 27 of keel. The bottom tube composing the apex of the triangle of the keel forks out and floor girders are connected to the two tubes which here form the bottom member of the keel.

The length of the cabin is only 7 ft. 6 in. A passage-way is left on the port side of the ship, so that communication is practicable between the two gondolas without passing through the cabin. It is entered by a door opening on to the passage; a window looks on to the passage and another is fitted in the fabric cover on the starboard side. A table is fitted to carry the instruments, above which is the switchboard, 16 in. by 16 in. (Plate No. 15.)

A duralumin tube in the floor provides means for lowering out the aerial without fouling any part of the ship. The winder for this is fitted immediately above it.

Fins, Rudders, and Elevators.

The systems of fins which give the ship the necessary stability in flight are two, viz., vertical and horizontal.

The vertical fin is composed of two parts, one above and one below the centre line of the hull. It is constructed of a frame of duralumin girders, suitably cross-braced and covered with single-ply titanine-doped fabric. The girders throughout are single-braced box girders. The fin is attached on one side to the transverse frames of the hull and is wire-braced from the other edge to the hull.

The vertical fin area of the ship is 1,100 sq. ft.

The two horizontal fins, in construction and attachment, are similar to the vertical fins, but, though termed "horizontal," there is a slight dihedral angle between the two fins, which helps to throw the water off in the event of the ship flying in rain.

The horizontal fin area is 2,140 sq. ft.

The triplane rudders and biplane elevators are of the "box" type. They are carried by a framework of duralumin tubes, in some places strengthened with wood. This framework is connected to the under side of the horizontal planes, and also in the centre to the bottom members at the end of the keel. The elevators are contained in the same framework and come below the rudders, two on each side of the centre line of the ship for practically the full width of the horizontal fins. (*See* Plate No. 16.)

The rudder and elevator planes are made up of duralumin sections diagonally wire-braced and covered with fabric. (*See* Plates Nos. 17 and 18.) The area of the rudders is 576 sq. ft., or 52·4 per cent. of the vertical fin area, while the area of the elevators is 480 sq. ft., which is 22·5 per cent. of the horizontal fin area.

Auxiliary biplane rudders were fitted originally at No. 16 transverse frame. They were balanced and situated on the port and starboard sides of the ship, being attached by tubular struts to the transverse frame and keel. The controls ran through pulleys without any gearing to the after car. The control wheel and pedestal were situated on the port side of the car. During both the first two trial flights these rudders proved very unsatisfactory, and it was decided to remove the whole system.

Tests of Horizontal Fins.

The horizontal fins were tested by loading them with planks of wood. The total load applied worked out at exactly 1 lb. per sq. ft. on the superficial area of the fins.

No perceptible deformation was noticed. The planks used weighed exactly 1 lb. per lineal foot, and they were set out 1 foot apart, centre to centre. They were fairly flexible and the load was applied well on to the cover, and was not taken merely by the girders of the framework.

Tests on Rudders and Elevators.

Backlash.—The rudders and elevators were found to have a considerable amount of backlash at the preliminary trial. The control wires aft of the reduction boxes were therefore in each

To face p. 18.

PLATE No. 16.

STERN VIEW OF SHIP, SHOWING FINS, ELEVATORS, AND RUDDERS.

PLATE No. 17.
ELEVATOR PLANE.

To face p. 19.

PLATE NO. 18. RUDDER PLANE.

case tightened up. At the final test it was found that they were both now considerably harder to work, but the backlash was only trifling. A protractor was rigged up on both rudders and elevators, and the indicators in the cars were marked for each 5° angle of inclination of the planes. The planes were in each case moved first one way and then in the reverse direction, and the 5° points marked in each case.

Two series of points were thus obtained on the indicators. The distance between these two marks for any particular angle of inclination of the rudder planes, compared with the space representing a motion of 5° travel of the planes, gives the total backlash of the planes. It was found that for the rudder planes the backlash was half a degree over the whole scale, while in the elevators the backlash was 2°. Owing to the overhung weight of the elevator planes, the tension, and thus the stretch of the wires, was greater. This accounts for the greater backlash. The distance between each of the two series of marks was bisected to give the final points for the graduation of the index plates.

Tests under Loading.

A load of 56 lbs. was applied at the trailing edge of each group of rudder planes in such a way that whichever way the planes were moved from the central position the load tended to bring them back to this position.

This is equivalent to a total torque of 672 lbs.-ft., and equivalent to 17½° inclination; the steering wheel became fairly stiff to turn and the backlash was greatly increased.

In the case of the elevators, a load of 30 lbs. was applied to the trailing edge on each side of the ship in a similar manner, with similar results. This torque equals 270 lbs.-ft., and is equivalent to 19° inclination at 50 m.p.h. As a result of this test, proposals were put forward to modify the controls so as to obtain—

(1) Greater leverage at the wheel by increasing the number of turns required for a given inclination of the planes.*

(2) A reduction of the strain in the control wires and so reduce the stretch under load.

(3) Elastic applied near the reduction box in order to draw the slack wire away from the car, so as to minimise the chance of the chain in the car jumping from the lower sprocket wheels, as occurred once during the test.†

---

* Subsequently done by means of pulleys and sheaves. (Ratio 2 : 1.)

† Subsequently done.

Turning Trials—H.M.A., R. No. 9.

29th September 1917.

Wind.—S., 5–10 knots.
Ship's head on putting helm over.—150°.
Angle turned through.—360°.

Direction of Turn.	Helm used.	Time taken to turn 360° (t).		Air Speed (by Indicator) (S).	Circumference of Turning Circle (D).	Radius of Turning Circle $\frac{D}{2\pi}$
	°	m.	s.	Knots.	Yards.	Yards.
Starboard* -	20	20	58	17	10,950	1,750
Port* - -	20	11	33	17	6,600	1,050
Starboard -	20	7	00	24	5,600	890
Port - -	20	6	33	24	5,240	840

Wind.—S. by W., 15 knots.

Direction of Turn.	Helm used.	m.	s.	Knots.	Yards.	Yards.
Starboard -	20	5	35	34	6,350	1,050
Port - -	20	5	17	34	5,800	930
Starboard -	10	5	35	34	6,350	1,050
Port - -	10	6	5	34	6,900	1,100

* In these turns the ship answered very erratically, and at one time actually started swinging in the reverse direction.

CHAPTER III.

Gasbags, Valves, and Fittings—Outer Cover—General Fabric Work.

Gasbags.

We have seen in the previous chapter that the hull of the ship is divided into 17 compartments, each containing a single gasbag. These will now be described in greater detail, together with the valves, outer cover, and fabric work in general.

It will be noticed that, in nearly every department of the ship, alterations had to be made to make the whole structure lighter in order to gain the disposable lift demanded by the terms of the contract. The gasbags themselves were no exception to the general rule.

The original bags were composed of single-ply cotton fabric, rubber-proofed, and lined inside with three layers of goldbeaters' skin.

H. M

ARRANGEME

F

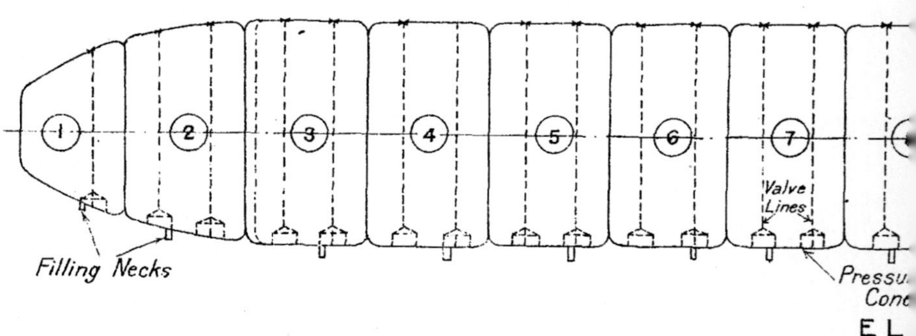

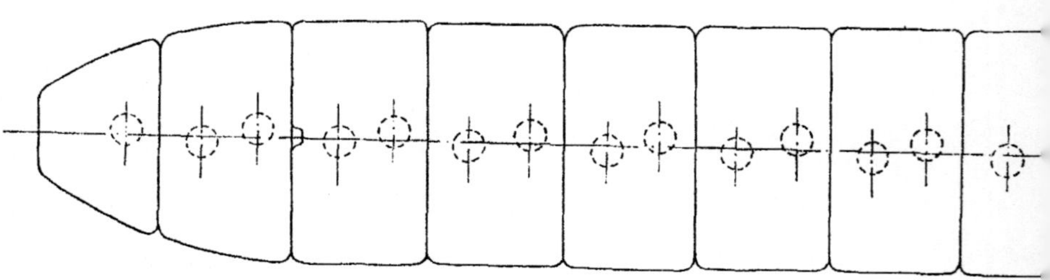

7271.

Nº 9.

F GASBAGS.

4.

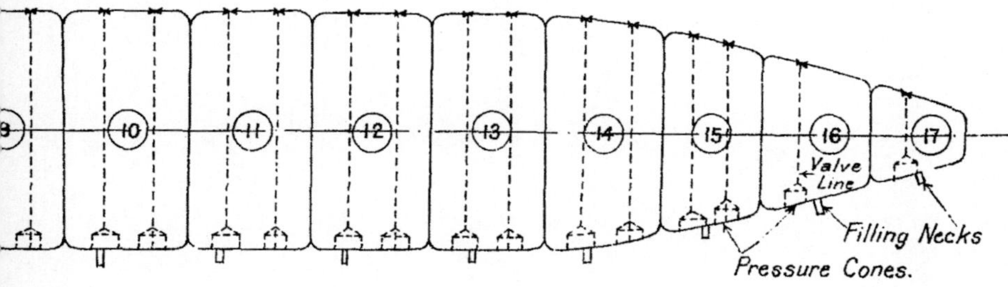

ION.

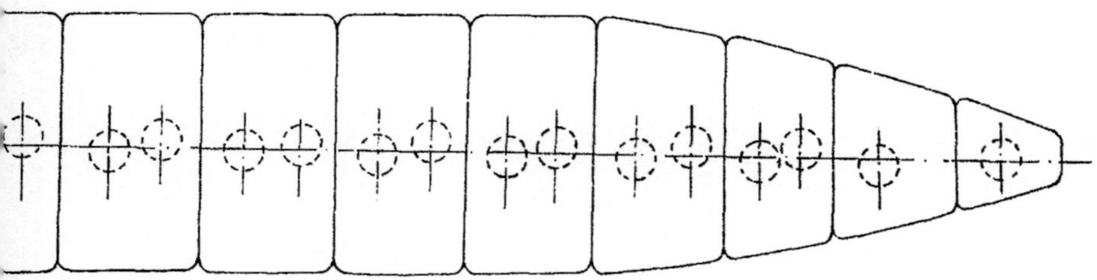

Malby & Sons, Lith.

	Grs. per Sq. Metre.
Weight of fabric	120
Weight of rubber	80
Weight of skin (three layers)	100
Total	300

Strength of fabric, 1,100 to 1,200 kgs. per sq. m.

The fabric was dyed yellow, and supplied by the Continental Tyre and Rubber Company.

After the initial trial flights, when the ship was laid up for alterations to the power units and attendant modifications of gondolas, &c., it was decided to substitute lighter bags for those originally used. The new bags were composed of single-ply cotton fabric, rubber-proofed on one face, with two layers of goldbeaters' skin, the weights being—

	Grs. per Sq. Metre.
Weight of fabric	120
Weight of rubber	40
Weight of skins (two layers)	70
Total	230

Strength of fabric, 1,100 kgs. per sq. m. both ways.

This resulted in a saving of weight to the extent of ·35 ton.

The following table gives the capacity of the bags :—

No. of Bag.	Capacity.
1	19,253
2	53,664
3 to 13	680,372 (61,852 each).
14	59,570
15	44,842
16	24,176
17	7,430
Total	889,307

Manufacture of Gasbags.

The following is a brief description of the various processes the bags go through in course of manufacture.

The fabric is supplied rubber-proofed and ready for use. It is then marked out from templates and cut to the required shapes. The gasbags are made in three main parts, namely :—

The circumferential portion.
The first or forward flat end.
The second or aft flat end.

The pieces for these portions having been cut out, are handed over to other operatives for joining up and seaming. The joining up is done so that one piece overlaps the adjoining piece by 20 mm. These overlapping portions are solutioned together, the seams being then stitched by an electrically driven machine with twin needles. To cover this stitching the seams are taped both sides, a tape of 40 mm. width being used. This tape is solutioned on each side of the seam, and, to render it gastight, the material of the tape is proofed both sides.

Filling necks, valve petticoats, pressure cones, and other details are cut out, seamed, and taped in the same manner, and as much work is done as is possible before the application of the goldbeaters' skin.

Goldbeaters' skin is used to render the gasbags as gastight as possible. It is made from the intestines of oxen and is practically entirely imported from America.

The skins have to be put through a preparatory process before being ready for use. They are first salted and then rinsed through four lots of lukewarm water to remove all dirt and extraneous matter. They are then placed in a bath of water and glycerine and scraped with a knife to remove all fat and make them as pure as possible. They are then ready for attaching to the fabric.

The skins are laid, the rough side downwards, on the rubbered side of the fabric, and are attached by a very thin coat of solution, overlapping at the joins approximately $1\frac{3}{4}$ in. The rough edges are trimmed off and the succeeding layer is placed in an opposite direction to the first.

The several portions of the gasbag are now ready for joining up. The seams are made in the ordinary way, care being taken that the skin is removed where the seam has to be made, as the rubber solution will not adhere to the skin.

When completed the bags are inflated with air to ensure that they are of right shape and dimension. (Plate No. 19.)

Fittings to Gasbags.

The gasbags are suspended from the top longitudinal frame of the hull in the following manner. Circular patches, 12 ins. diameter, of 2-ply balloon fabric, are attached to the gasbags by rubber solution. A piece of webbing 2 ins. wide is stitched to the bottom ply of the patch. The top ply, which covers the webbing, is stuck on over the patch. A leather strap passes through the webbing and is attached to a duralumin stirrup, which is riveted on to the channel member of the longitudinal girder. There are eight suspension patches to all the bags except No. 17, to which there are only six.

A small observation window is fitted to each bag. The frame of the window consists of two aluminium rings 82 mm. diameter, which are bolted together with brass bolts and nuts. A fabric washer is inserted to render the joint gastight, the window itself, 50 mm. diameter, being composed of cellon.

To face p. 22.

Plate No. 19.
Gasbag.

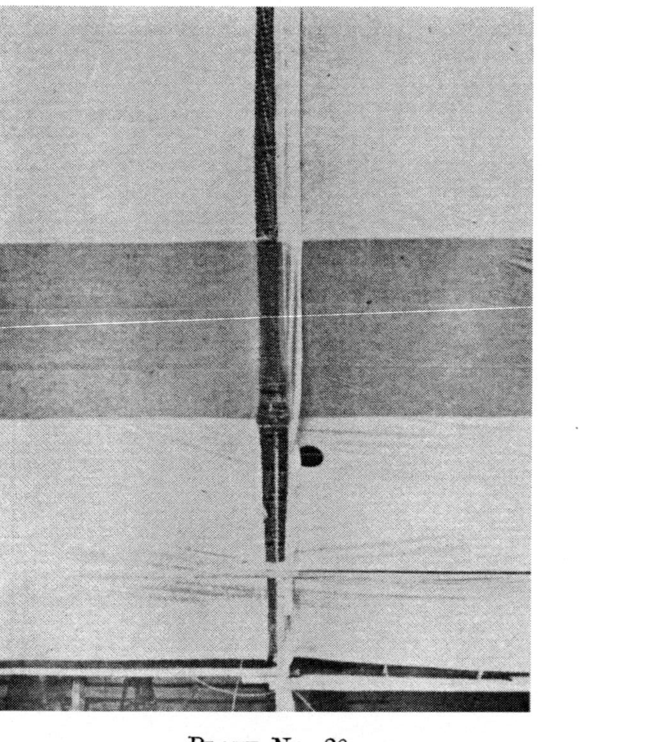

PLATE NO. 20.

SHOWING METHOD OF LACING OLD OUTER COVER WITH STRAIGHT EDGE.

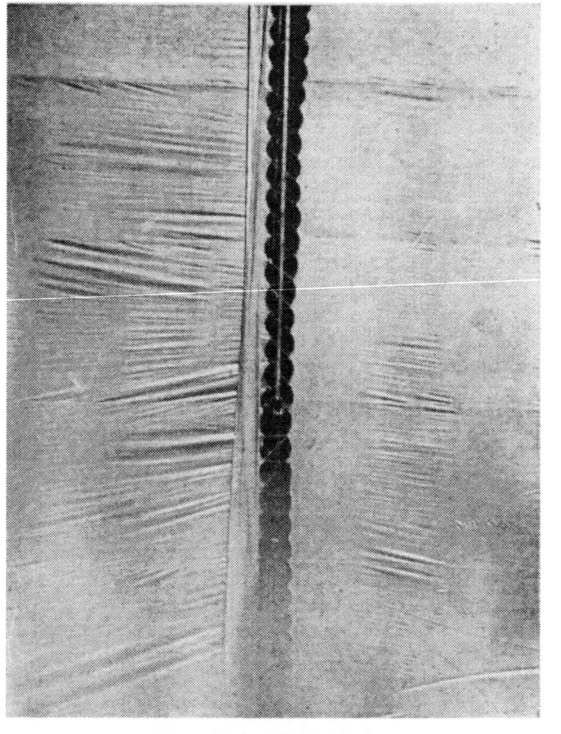

PLATE NO. 21.

SHOWING METHOD OF LACING NEW OUTER COVER WITH SCALLOPED EDGE.

To face p. 22.

PLATE No. 22.

OUTER COVER READY FOR LACING

Filling Necks.—The inner neck, 1 ft. 4 in. diameter, is made of single-ply fabric skinned; the outer neck, 1 ft. 8 in. diameter, is single-ply fabric unskinned. The cover to these is of 2-ply fabric.

The pressure and purity connections consist of a $\frac{3}{8}$-in. diameter fabric tube, cut and turned back 2 ins. and stuck on to a two-ply fabric patch 6 in. diameter, stuck on the inside of the gasbag.

Outer Cover.

The object of the outer cover is to cover the whole framework of the ship, to protect the gasbags and the hull framework from the weather, to render the outer surface of the ship symmetrical, and reduce "skin friction" and resistance to the air to a minimum.

To enable the cover to be easily handled and removed, if necessary, for repairs to framework, &c., it is made in two parts, a port and starboard side to each gasbag. Aluminium eyelets are attached to the edges, which are suitably strengthened for the purpose. The eyeletted edges permit of one section being laced to the next; the sections being all laced together form the complete cover. The top edges of all sections are laced to the walking-way, while the bottom edges are laced to the keel of the ship. (Plates Nos. 20, 21, and 22.)

Rubber solution is not used for joining the seams. A special seam is adopted, in which the edges of the fabric are folded inside the seam itself. This seam is folded automatically by the machine which stitches the fabric with twin needles. All seams are so arranged that they shed water. To do this the loose edges must always point towards the bottom.

To prevent as much as possible penetration of heat from the sun, which would cause the gas in the bags to expand and the pressure to increase, the fabric of the upper half of the ship is impregnated with aluminium dust. Ordinary doped fabric is used for most of the other parts. Special fireproofed fabric is used for the portions of the cover above the gondolas, and also adjoining the gun platform. This reduces the danger of fire from sparks or heat.

The diagram shows clearly the doping scheme for the whole outer cover. (Fig. 5.)

The cover is made of linen fabric doped with cellulose acetate.

Weight of linen	-	$2\frac{1}{2}$ ozs. per sq. yd.
Strength	- -	50 lbs. per sq. in.
Weight of dope	-	$1\frac{1}{2}$ ozs. per sq. yd. (approx.) for aluminium-coated.
		$1\frac{1}{4}$ ozs. per sq. yd. for plain doping.

For the bow sheets the linen weight is $3\frac{1}{2}$ ozs. per sq. yd.

Strength	- -	70 lbs. per sq. in.

Covering strips of thin holland were laced to the longitudinal girders to prevent chafing of the gasbags. A $1\frac{1}{2}$-mm. cord runs along the outside edges of these strips, to which the holland is stitched, and $\frac{3}{16}$-in. eyelets to take the lacing cords are placed as close to the edges as possible.

The top walking-way was found to be wearing badly before the ship left Barrow. A new fabric covering was attached, made of canvas, with fabric edges for sticking to the outer cover.

During the initial trial flight the outer cover flapped badly in the after part of the ship in the wake of the after propellers. This was remedied by sewing a lacing strip to the cover and attaching it to the G, H, and J girders where necessary. The cover was also laced at these places to the Mallock tubes, and, to further secure it to the hull framework, a patch was stitched to the cover and attached to the bracing wires where they intersect in each panel formed by the girders and the Mallock tubes.

Identification Marks.

The following are the identification marks and their disposition on the ship :—

Outer Cover of Hull.—Alternate rings of red, white, and blue on the extreme nose and tail of the ship.

Between Nos. 8 and 9 transverse frames on top of ship, and also between the F and H longitudinal girders on port and starboard sides, to be visible from underneath, red, white, and blue circles, the diameter of the whole being about 18 ft., with the centres of the circles red.

Horizontal Fins.—Similar red, white, and blue circles, about 15 ft. diameter, on top of fins.

Elevators.—Alternate red, white, and blue stripes on the under side.

Rudders.—Alternate red, white, and blue vertical stripes on the two outer edges, port and starboard.

Large figures 9 in black, level with the axis of the hull, one between Nos. 2 and 3 transverse frames, the other just forward of the horizontal planes on both port and starboard sides.

Gas Valves and Fittings.

Two gas valves are fitted to each gasbag, one entirely automatic, the other automatic but also controlled by hand.

The valves are attached to the gasbag by the ordinary valve petticoat, the hole in the bag being 22¼ ins. in diameter.

The valves are fitted to the tops of the bags, the hand-controlled valve being in each case aft of the automatic one. The valve is connected by a shackle to a duralumin supporting arm riveted to the walking-way girder, which is the top longitudinal member of the hull. From this attachment runs a central steel tubular strut from which the valve is stayed by six duralumin wires, three on the top and three on the bottom, evenly spaced. (Plate No. 24.)

The valve seating is composed of an aluminium channel with a rubber seating, this being held in place by a fabric strapping.

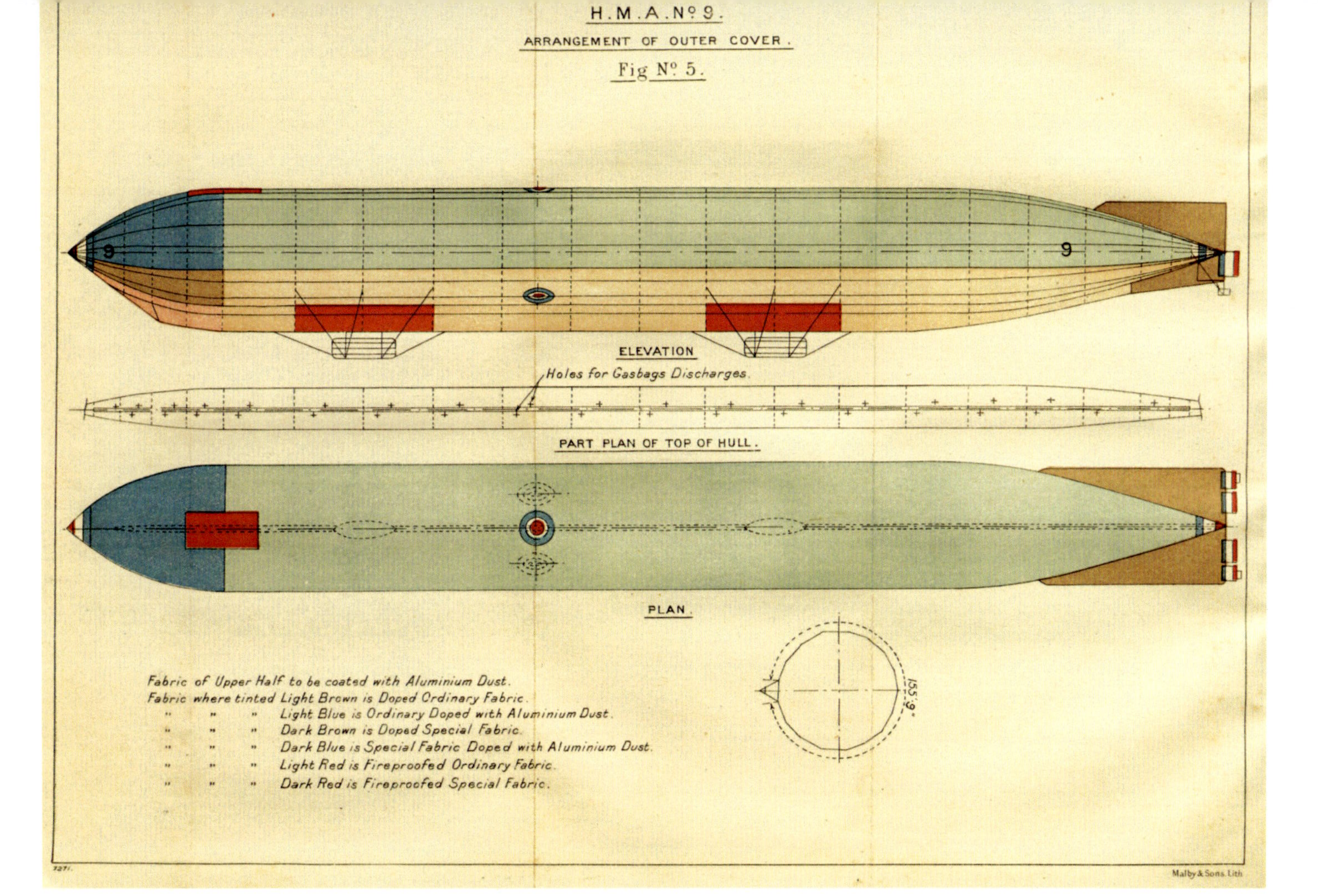
H.M.A.No 9.
ARRANGEMENT OF OUTER COVER.
Fig No 5.
9
9
ELEVATION
Holes for Gasbags Discharges.
PART PLAN OF TOP OF HULL.
PLAN.
155'9"
Fabric of Upper Half to be coated with Aluminium Dust.
Fabric where tinted Light Brown is Doped Ordinary Fabric.
" " " Light Blue is Ordinary Doped with Aluminium Dust.
" " " Dark Brown is Doped Special Fabric.
" " " Dark Blue is Special Fabric Doped with Aluminium Dust.
" " " Light Red is Fireproofed Ordinary Fabric.
" " " Dark Red is Fireproofed Special Fabric.
Malby & Sons. Lith.

Plate No. 23. Top Valve.

Plate No. 24.
Top Valve, showing Attachment to Walking-way Girder.

PLATE No. 25.
AUTOMATIC SIDE VALVE.

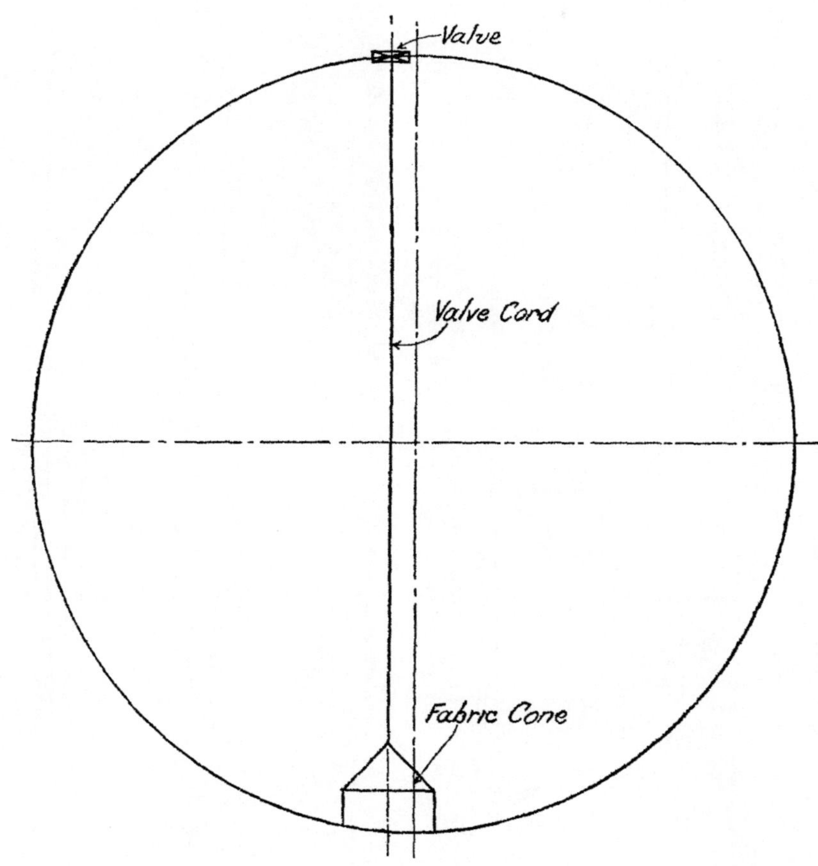

Fig. No. 6.

Diagrammatic Sketch showing Method of Operating Automatic Valves.

To face p. 25.

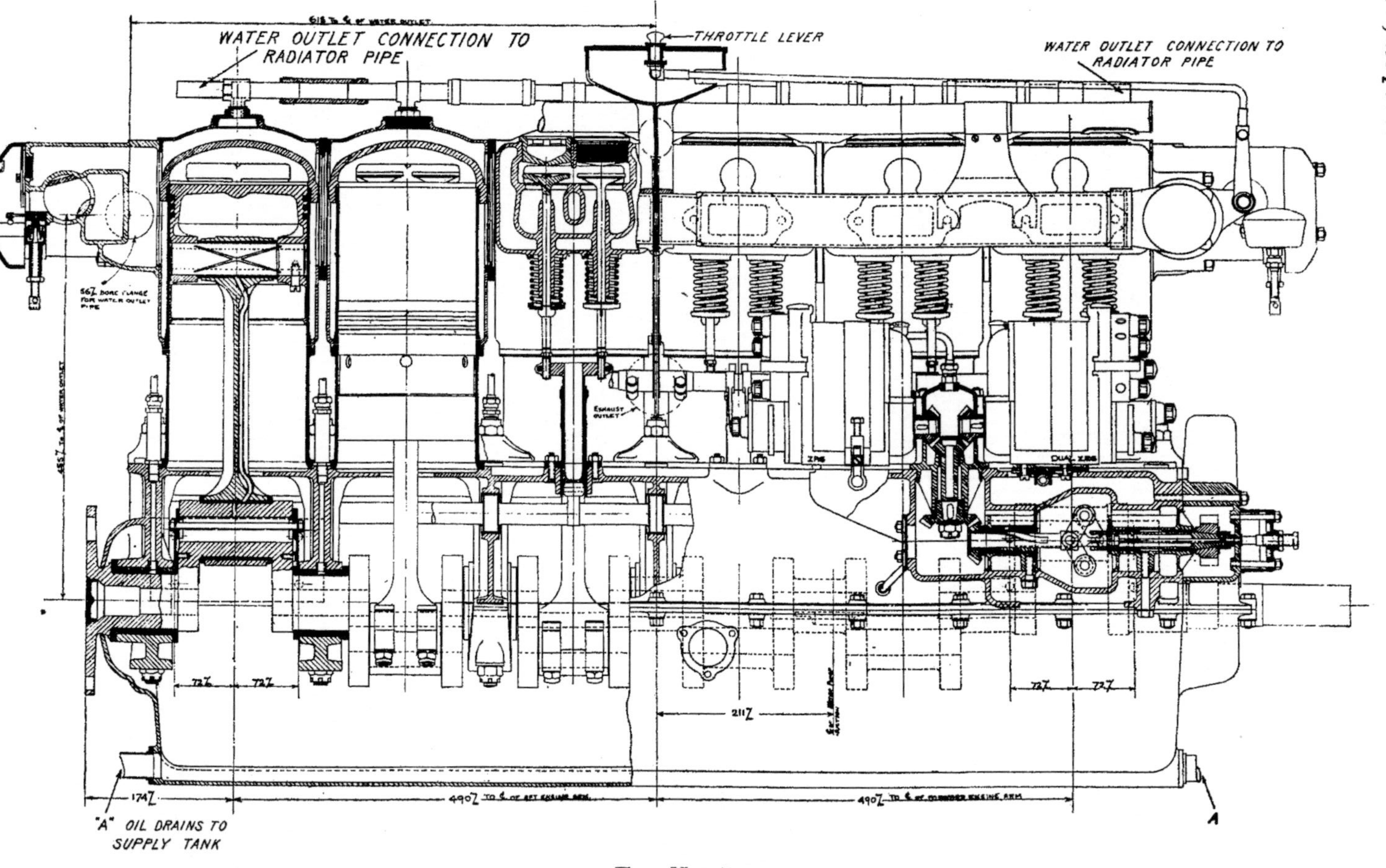

FIG. NO. 7.
SECTION OF WOLSELEY-MAYBACH ENG NE.

The top and bottom valve-retaining rings are of wood bolted together.

Six springs of steel wire, standard wire gauge 33, keep the valve closed.

To open the valve, six flexible steel wire ropes, $\frac{1}{4}$ in. circumference, attached to lugs, meet at a steel socket to which the valve rope is secured. From the same socket a wire rope is attached to the central strut, and limits the opening of the valve to $3\frac{1}{2}$ ins.

The valve rope itself is of hemp, $\frac{3}{4}$ in. circumference.

To take the escaping gas from the valves of bags Nos. 1, 2, and 3 clear of the gun mounted on the top of the hull, trunks were originally designed. These were found exceptionally difficult to fit, and it was decided, after the trial flights had been carried out, to fit automatic side valves of the Zeppelin type, as are fitted in H.M.A., R. No. 23. (Plate No. 25.)

This caused the automatic valves of bags Nos. 2 and 3 to be removed, one being left in each bag to be hand-controlled. The existing valve in bag No. 1 was retained to serve the same purpose.

Pressure Cones.

The pressure cones, by means of which the valves are automatically controlled, are fitted to the bottoms of the bags. These cones are composed of three parts, all made of two-ply balloon fabric, the upper and lower fabric cones and the fabric socket, which is attached to the bottom of the bag.

The cone is kept circular in plan by means of two laminated wood rings at the connections of the upper and lower fabric cones and the lower cones and the socket.

CHAPTER IV.

Engines—Transmission—Propellers—Petrol System—Fire Prevention.

Engines of H.M.A., R. No. 9.

The engine equipment of H.M.A., R. No. 9 was originally composed of four Wolseley Maybach engines, each of 180-h.p., two units being situated in the foremost gondola and two in the after gondola. (*See* Plate No. 27.)

The deficiency of disposable lift observed in the ship on the occasion of the lift trial of November 21st, 1916, was in part remedied by radical modifications of the engine equipment of the after gondola. Originally the engines of both cars drove swivelling propellers, but it was ultimately decided to—

1. Remove both engines of the after car and replace them with a single engine of 250-h.p.

2. Remove the swivelling propeller gear of the after car.

3. Replace the swivelling propellers of the after car by one directly-driven propeller astern of the car.

4. Remove the reverse gear box from the after gondola and place it in the foremost gondola.

5. Modify the shape of the after car in order to make it suitable for the single propeller.

The 180-H.P. Wolseley Maybach Engine.

This engine is similar to the German-made engines of this horse power which were installed in H.M.A., P. Nos. 4, 6, and 7.

For H.M.A., R. No. 9, the 180-h.p. engines were constructed by Messrs. Wolseley Motors, Limited, and are almost an exact copy of the German-made engine of this type, the chief differences being in the crank shaft, petrol pump, water circulation and connecting rods, such differences being comparatively small, but their sum-total making the engine slightly heavier than the German-made engine.

The following are the chief features of this engine :—

(1) Six-cylinder, vertical.
(2) Four valves per cylinder (two inlet, two exhaust).
(3) Two carburettors per engine.
(4) Two sparking plugs per cylinder.
(5) Two separate magneto ignition circuits.
(6) Automatic ignition advance mechanism.
(7) Automatic cut-out for the ignition if engine exceeds 1,450 r.p.m.
(8) Automatic cut-out for the ignition if the oil pressure drops below 10 lbs. per square inch.
(9) Method of engine starting.

The special features can be observed probably better from the drawing (Fig. No. 7) than from any description, but with regard to the method of starting this engine a few words may be explanatory. A lever, which is not shown in the diagram, is pulled to the downward position. This operation lifts both the exhaust valves and the inlet valves off their seatings, and connects the hand-starting pump (not shown in the general arrangement diagrams) to the exhaust pipe. On working the hand pump air is sucked through the carburettors, through the lifted inlet valves, and out to the pump through the lifted exhaust valves. When the pump has been worked for a few seconds by hand, the valves are allowed to drop on to their seatings by releasing the lever. A hand-operated magneto is connected to the engine magneto distributors, the throttle opened to a suitable position, and the hand magneto operated. This will give a spark in a cylinder in a position to fire, and in all probability will give the necessary impulse for starting the engine. Should it fail to do this, the same procedure is commenced again.

Fig. 9.

FORWARD ENGINE.

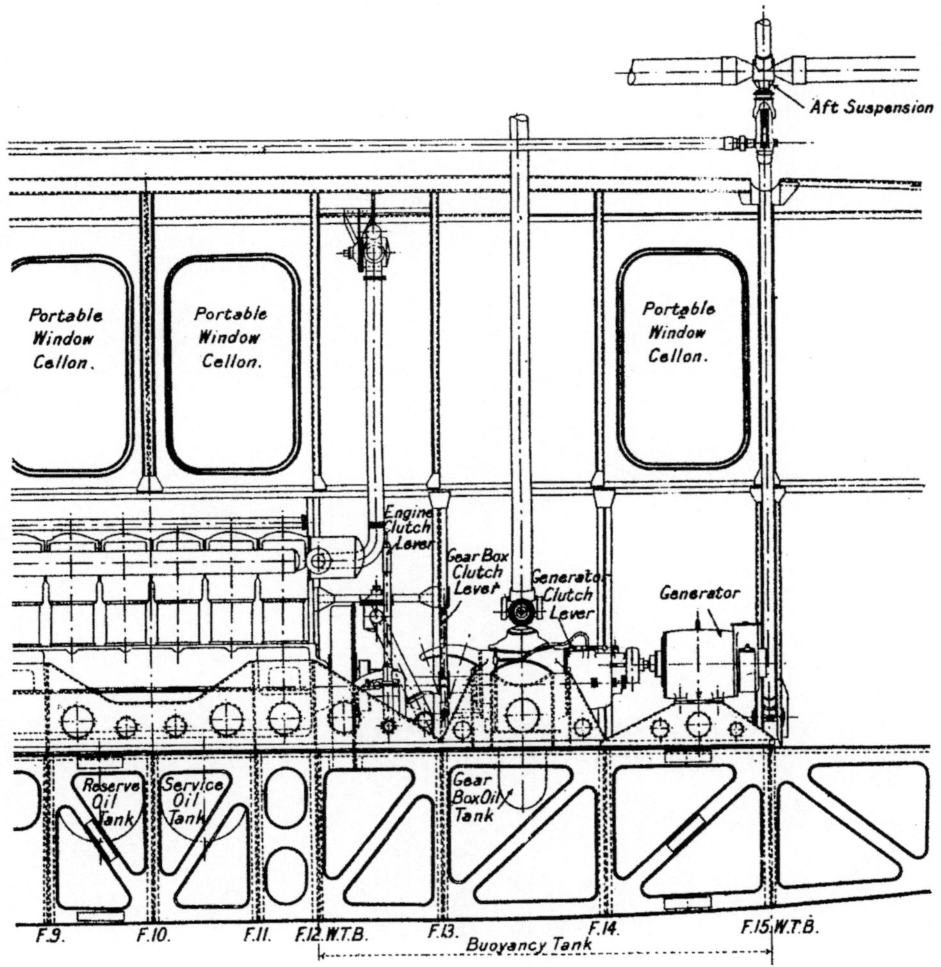

7351. 17869. Pk 2895. 250. 5. 18.

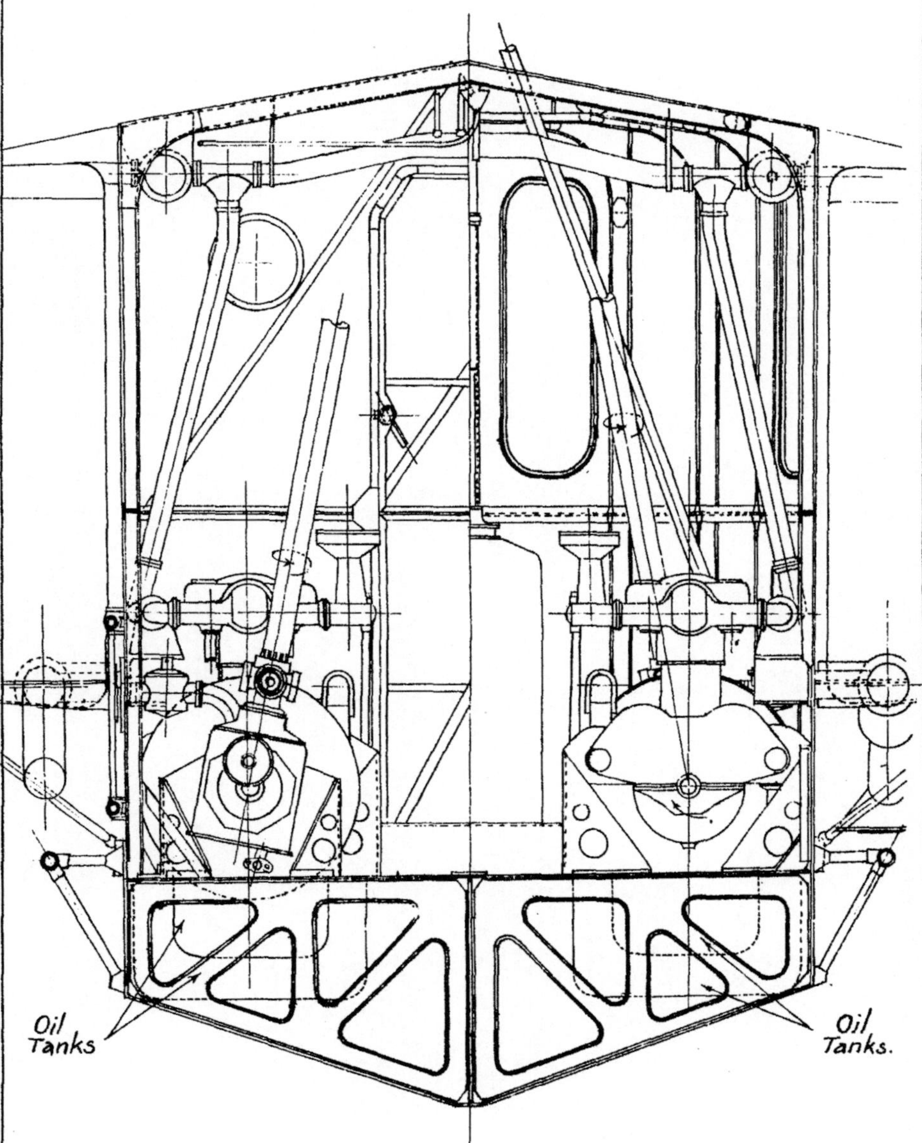

7271.

Malby & Sons. Lith

Plate No. 26.

180-h.p. Wolseley-Maybach Engine.

Plate No. 27.

Engines in position. Forward Car.

PLATE No. 28. FORWARD CAR, SHOWING SWIVELLING PROPELLERS.

To face p. 27.

Plate No. 29.

Swivelling Control Shaft for Propellers, Forward Car

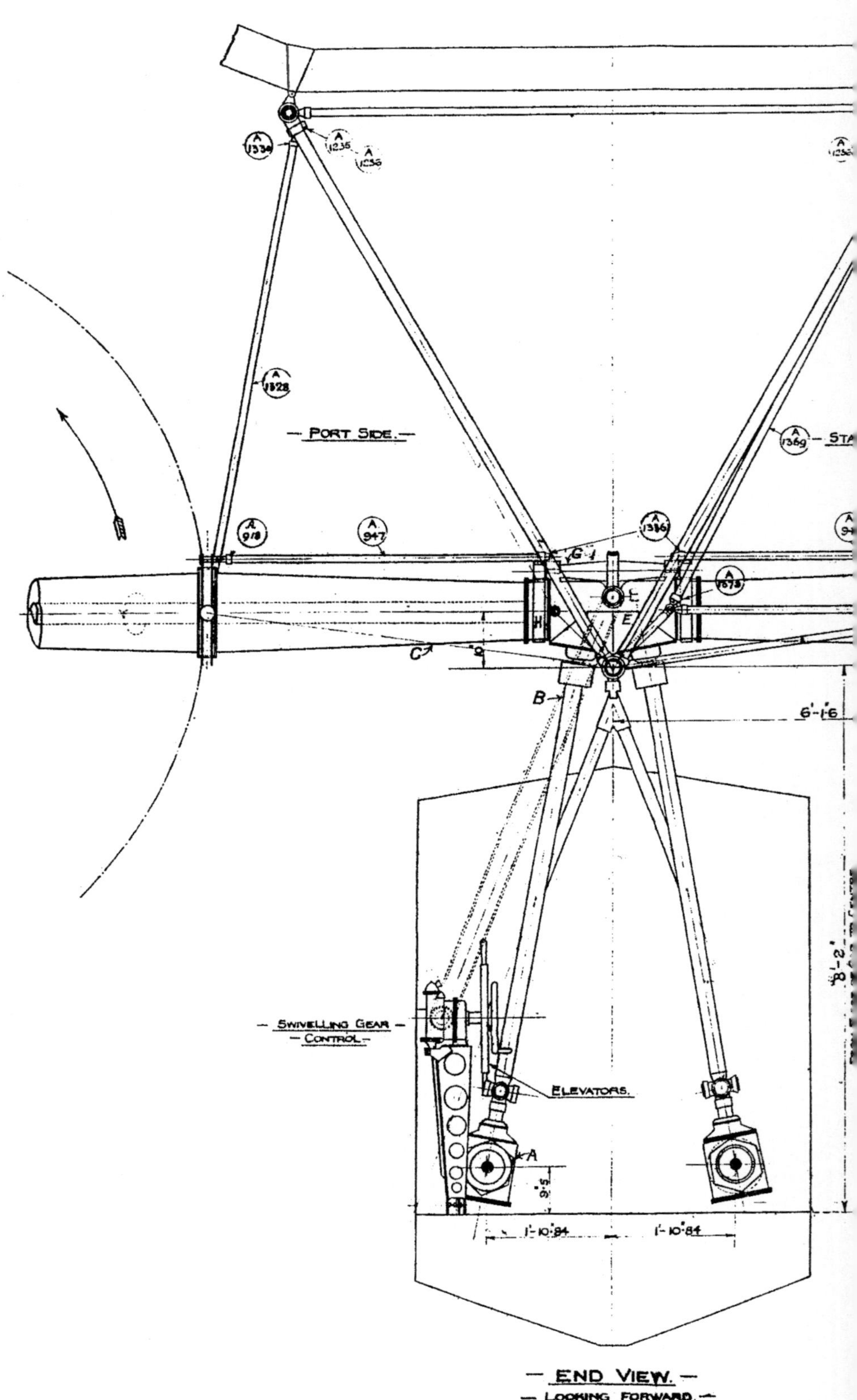

7351. 17869. Pt 2895.

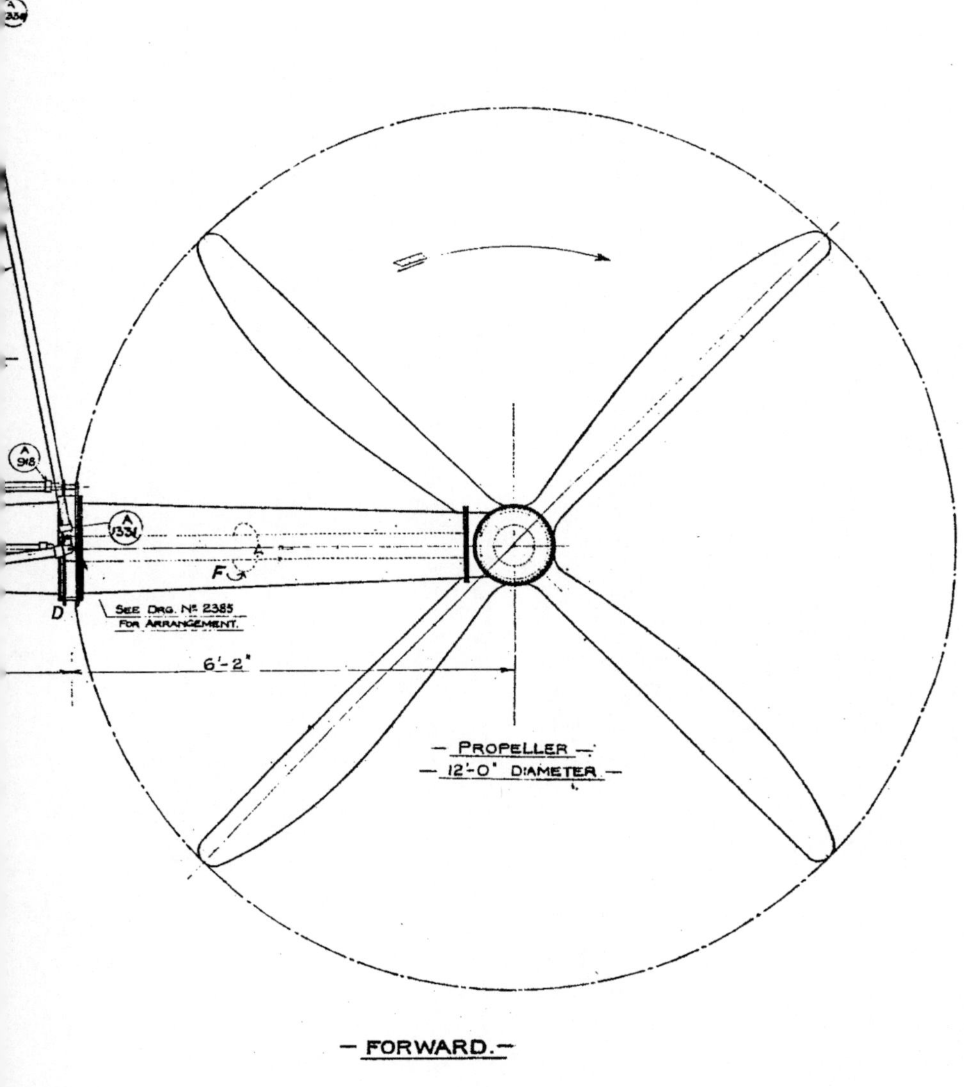

— FORWARD. —

ARRANGEMENT OF SWIVELLING PROPELLER GEAR.

FIG. Nº 8.

Malby & Sons. Lith.

Before using the hand-operated pump, the automatic oil pressure switch-off mechanism must be temporarily put out of action until the engine is started.

The *principal dimensions* of the 180-h.p. engine are :—

Bore, 160 mm. - - - - - =6·299 in.
Stroke, 170 mm. - - - - =6·693 in.
Normal h.p. at 1,200 r.p.m. - - - =180 b.h.p.
Maximum h.p. at 1,200 r.p.m. - - =188 b.h.p.
Maximum h.p. at 1,250 r.p.m. - - =190 b.h.p.
Maximum r.p.m. at which ignition cut-out operates - - - - - - - 1,350 to 1,450
Minimum r.p.m. at which oil indicator cuts off ignition - - - - - - - 400 to 500

The correct *valve Timing* is :—

Inlet opens 5° after top centre.
Inlet closes 30° after bottom centre.
Exhaust opens 46° before bottom centre.
Exhaust closes 15° after top centre.

Ignition Timing.—With the ignition fully retarded, fire top dead centre.

Transmission Gear—Forward Car. (Figs. 8 and 9.)

The power from both engines to the propellers is first transmitted by a leather clutch and short horizontal shaft from each engine running parallel to each other to the lower reduction gear box A. These lower gear boxes contain bevel gearing in the ratio of 27 : 30, and are also fitted with reverse wheels of the same ratio engaged by means of a sliding square clutch shaft and hand-operating lever. The gear-box casings are bolted to suitable plate bearers attached to the deck plating of the car.

The larger bevels are fitted on the end of the carden or vertical countershaft universal joints B, which are led at an angle through the car roof and end in a common mitre wheel gear box mounted in the centre of the transverse swivelling tube ; both these boxes are lubricated by jet lubrication, a small Albany pump being driven from the horizontal shaft of lower gear box, oil being supplied from a tank fitted under the deck of car. The swivelling tube C above the car is supported at the centre gear box E, and at 5 ft. 3 in. from the ends of the tube by ball bearings D, the outer ring of these bearings being held in position by thrust, torque, and suspension tubes from the keel. (Plate No. 29.)

The centre of the swivelling tube contains the bearings, housings, and transmission shaft F, which has a universal joint at each end actuating the propellers through the outer reduction gear boxes which are secured to each end of the tube. The reduction ratio of the boxes is 23 : 37.

Taking the engine speed at 1,200 revs., the speed of the four-bladed 12-ft. propellers is 600 r.p.m.

The swivelling tubes and outer propeller boxes are mounted in such a manner that both the weight of the propellers and the torque of engine are fairly balanced in all positions and at all powers. This condition is brought about by means of a lay shaft G, lying above the centre gear box and engaging each of the swivelling tubular members at its inner end by a plain spur reduction wheel H. The weights of propellers are balanced owing to the starboard propeller being placed forward of, and the port propeller aft of, their respective swivelling tubes, thus also enabling the torque values in the transmission shafts to be equal and opposite in sign.

The transmission gears to both engines are totally independent and only work in concert during one operation, *i.e.*, swivelling the propellers. The propellers in swivelling travel upon a true circular path round the transverse shafts.

The rotation of the tube is directly actuated by the two spurs referred to above, fitted one on each side of the centre gear box, but attached to the swivelling tube casing. The lay shaft carries midway in its length a worm wheel, the driving worm for which is led away by a duralumin extension tube to the forward end of the car and there connected by sprocket wheels and chain to a handwheel and pedestal inside the car; 16 revolutions of the handwheel giving one revolution of the swivelling tube.

250-H.P. Engine.

The engine of this type fitted to No. 9 was recovered from the German Zeppelin L 33 wrecked in England, and is a type of airship engine evolved by the Germans during the war. It is really a modification of the engine already described, possessing practically all the original features of the former. It is larger in size :—

Bore, 150 mm.,
Stroke, 180 mm.;

and the valves, which are of the overhead type, instead of being four in number per cylinder, are five—three exhaust and two inlet.

This engine as originally made was specially designed for large output of power at high altitudes, *i.e.*, its compression was very high (compression clearance ratio, $6\frac{1}{4}:1$). However, for use in H.M.A., R. No. 9—a ship not capable of long flight at high altitudes—it was decided that the clearance volumes of the cylinders should be increased. This was effected by making the tops of the pistons concave, giving an increase in clearance volume of 100 c.c. per cylinder. This reduces the output of power by about 20 h.p., but it makes a more suitable engine for work at low altitudes.

Transmission Gear—After Car. (Fig. No. 11.)

The drive from the single engine fitted to the after car to the transmission gear is made flexible between the engine and

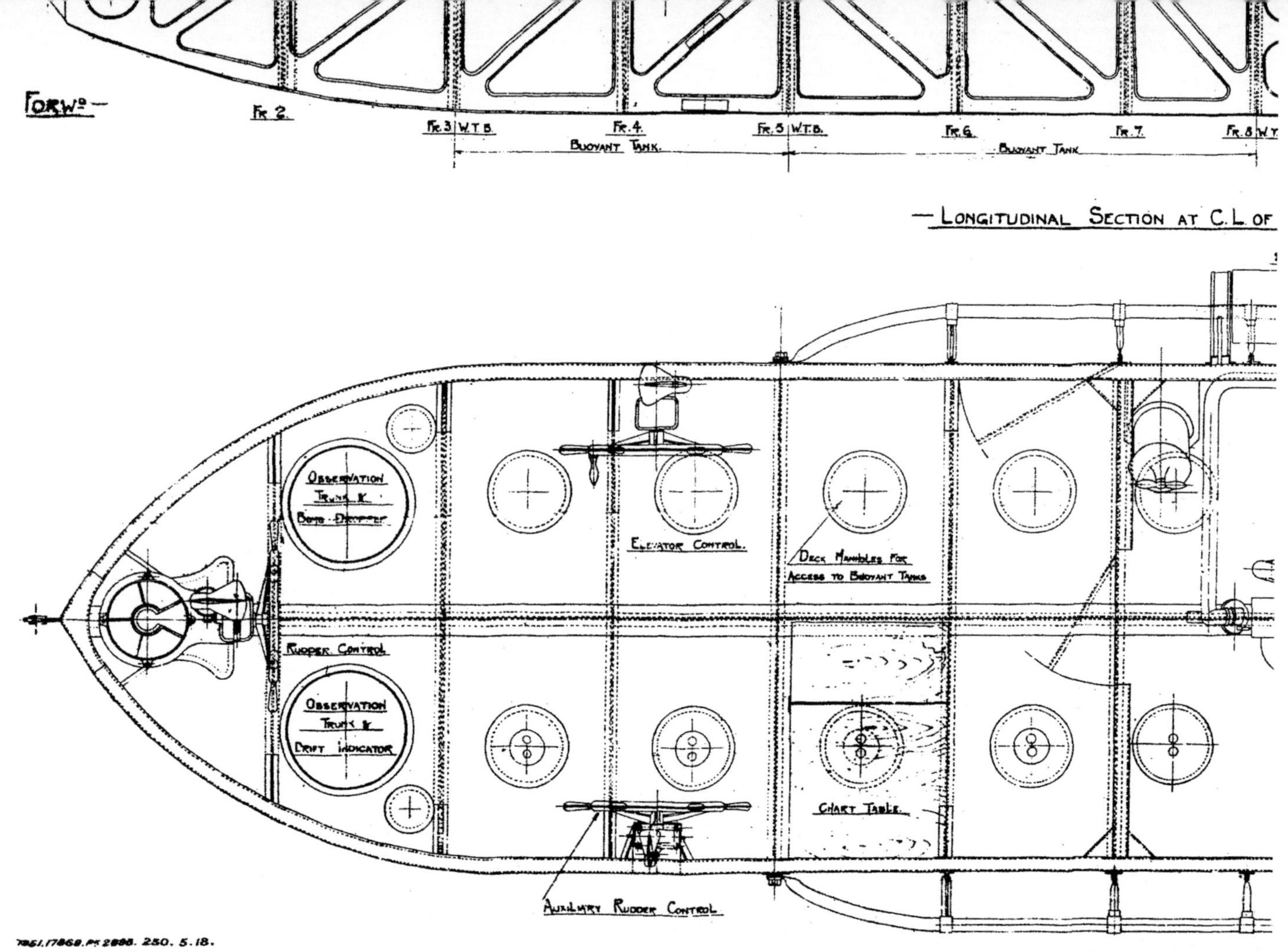

Forwᴰ
Fr. 2.
Fr. 3 W.T.B.
Fr. 4.
Fr. 5 W.T.B.
Fr. 6.
Fr. 7.
Fr. 8 W.T.
Buoyant Tank.
Buoyant Tank
— Longitudinal Section at C.L. of
Observation Trunk & Bomb Dropper
Observation Trunk & Drift Indicator
Rudder Control
Elevator Control.
Deck Manholes for Access to Buoyant Tanks
Chart Table.
Auxiliary Rudder Control
7861.17868. Pt 2886. 250. 5.18.

GENERAL ARRANGEMENT OF AFT CAR 4L. WITH ZEPPELIN MACHINERY.

FIG. No. 11.

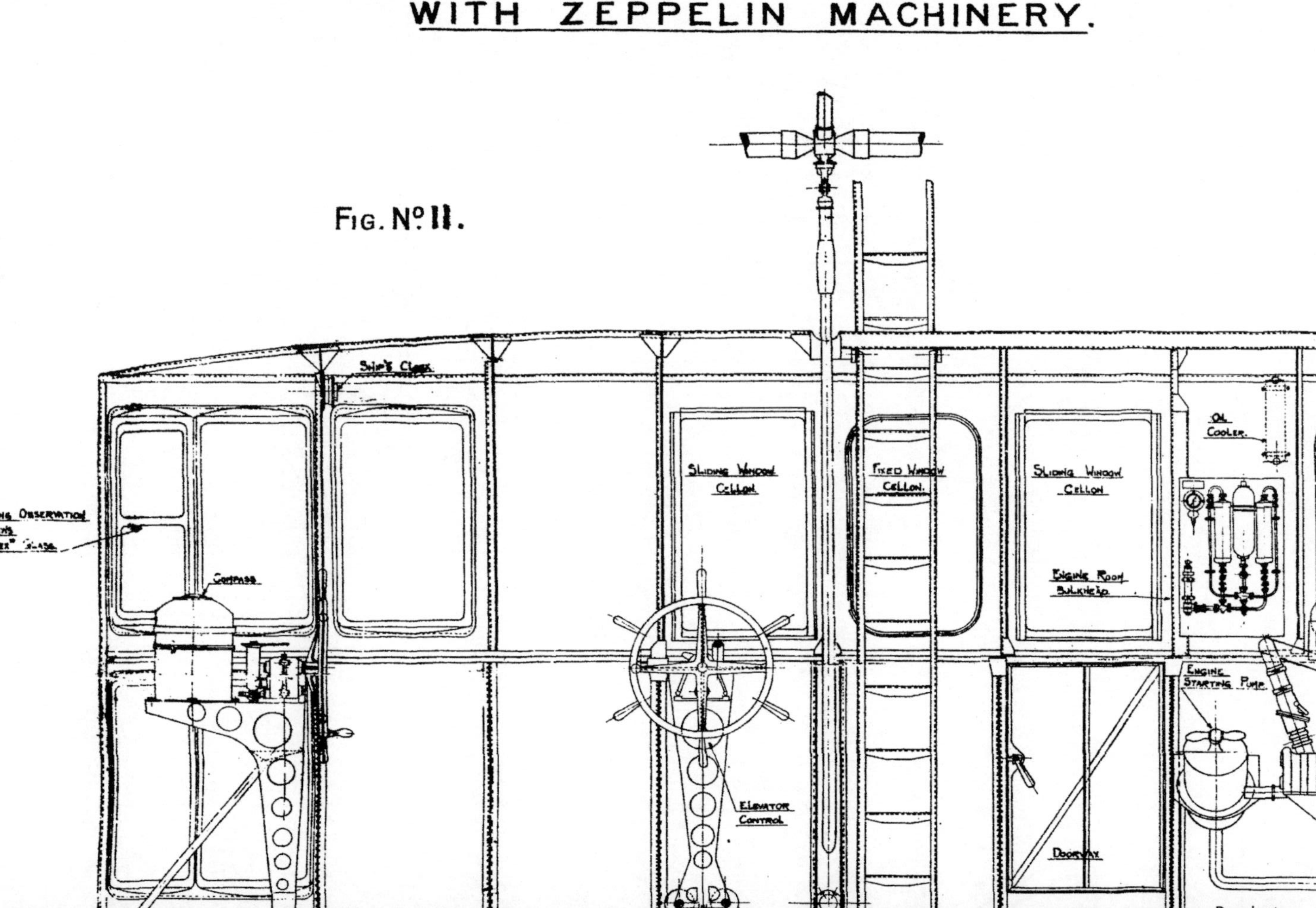

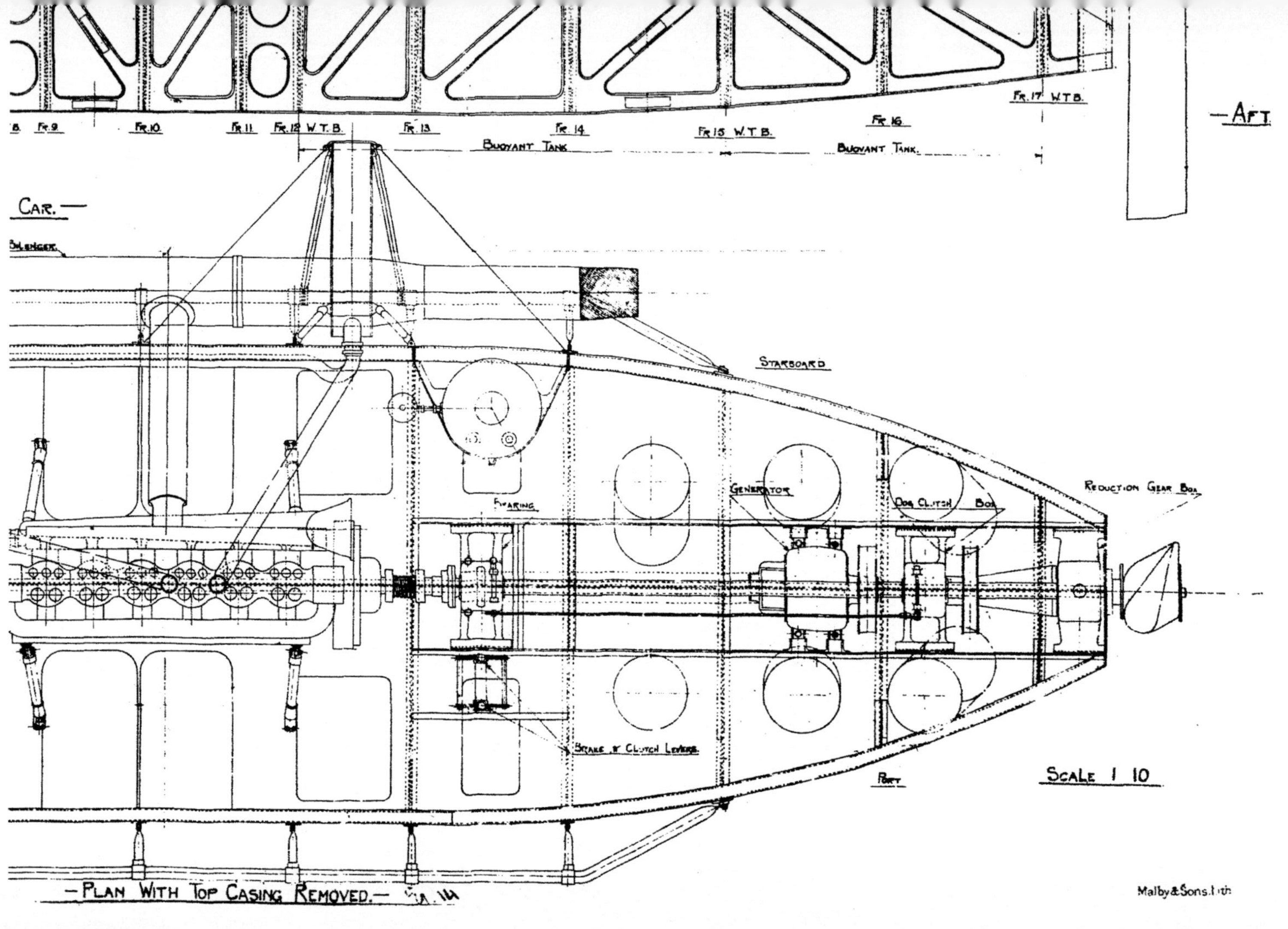
Fr. 9
Fr. 10
Fr. 11
Fr. 12 W.T.B.
Fr. 13
Fr. 14
Fr. 15 W.T.B.
Fr. 16
Fr. 17 W.T.B.
Buoyant Tank
Buoyant Tank
–Aft.
Car.–
Starboard
Fairing
Generator
Dog Clutch Box
Reduction Gear Box
Brake & Clutch Levers
Port
Scale 1 10
–Plan With Top Casing Removed.–
Malby & Sons. Lith.

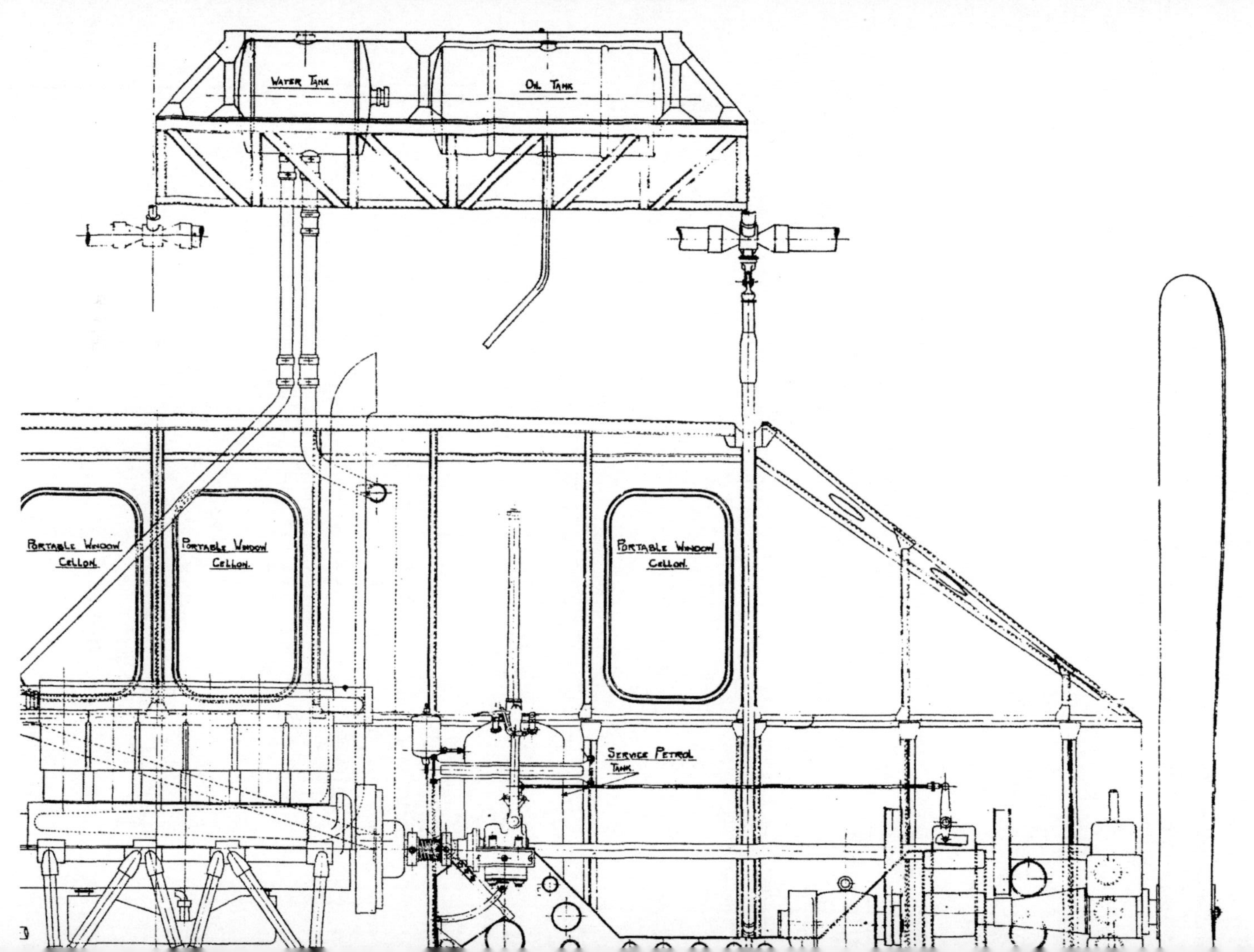

Water Tank
Oil Tank
Portable Window
Cellon.
Portable Window
Cellon.
Portable Window
Cellon.
Service Petrol
Tank.

H.M.

ARRG^T OF PETROL T

F

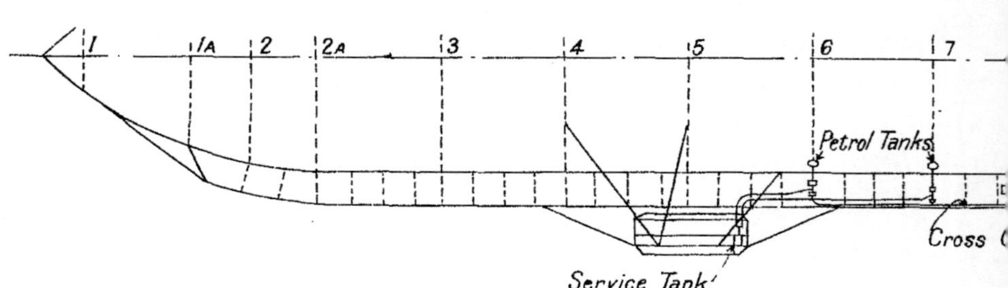

DIAGRAMMATIC ARRANGEMENT

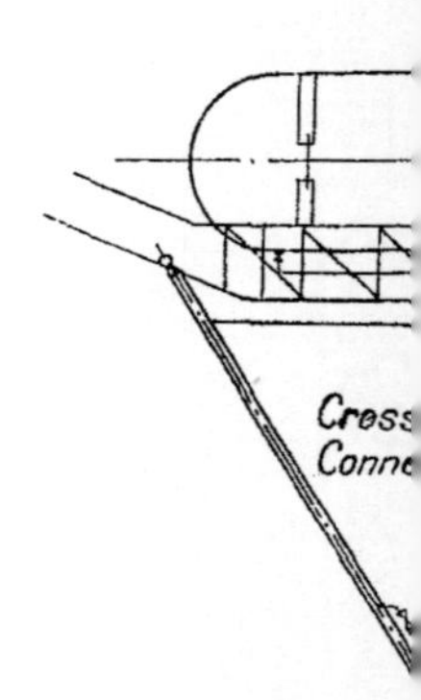

ARRANGEMENT

& CONNECTI

Nos 7 & 12

7871.

º 9.

& PIPE SYSTEM.

2.

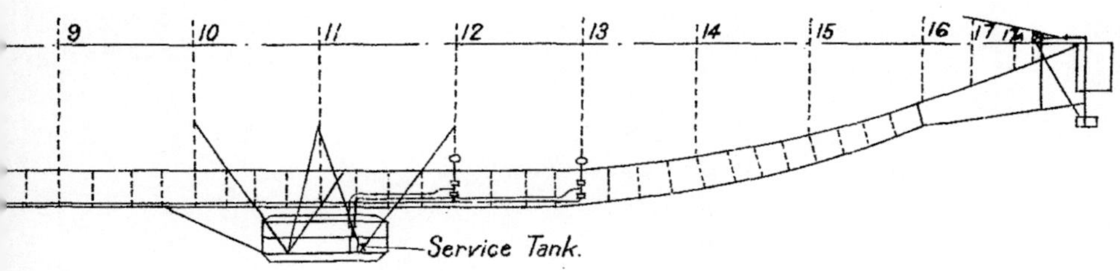

TROL PIPE LEADS FROM TANKS.

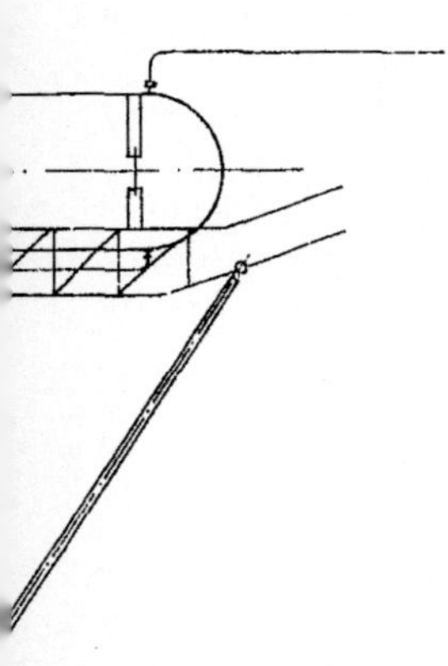

:TROL PIPES

FRAMES.

G AFT.

Malby & Sons, Lith.

shaft by vulcanised fibre blocks fitted between the flywheel and clutch casing.

The clutch is of the Hele-Shaw type A, carrying 11 bronze and 11 steel friction plates.

The load to the plates is supplied by a single spring loaded to 1,300 lbs. when compressed, actuated by a lever and two eccentrics.

The shaft running from the clutch ends in a coupling, and is coupled to a second shaft B, carrying a brake drum and pinion wheel. The pinion wheel gears into a spur mounted on a counter-shaft, the reducing value of the gears being in the ratio of 17 : 44. These are mounted on ball bearings and housed in an aluminium casing, and the shaft is extended aft on the centre of the car to drive the 17-ft. two-bladed propeller.

The engine clutch and the propeller brake are operated from the starting end of the engine.

Lubrication of Transmission Gear.

The bottom and top of the transmission from each engine gear box in the forward car is lubricated by means of a gear-driven pump driven off the main spindle of the gear box. This pump circulates the oil to the bearings of wheels in the gear box from an oil tank beneath the floor of the gondola. This oil during its circuit passes outside the gondola through a small radiator, whereby it is kept suitably cooled. The gear box at the end of the swivelling arm is lubricated by a gear pump fitted with its own oil supply.

Oil Service.

In the forward gondola the supply of lubricating oil to the engine is kept in four tanks beneath the floor of the gondola. (Figs. 9 and 10.) One tank beneath each engine is a reserve tank, while the other is a supply tank. The oil passes from the service tank to the piston pump in the engine, which distributes it throughout the engine bearings, and thence back into the service tank. A removable gauze strainer is interposed between the reservoir and the pump to strain the oil, and small strainers are fitted in the connection to each main bearing on the top face of the crank case. The oil in the service tank is also circulated through a gear-driven pump at the forward end of the engine through a radiator outside the car, and thence back to the service tank. In this way the oil temperature is kept reasonably low.

Petrol Service.

The petrol supply of the ship is arranged in tanks, which are situated on special girders composing the base of the transverse frame at frames 6, 7, 12, and 13. (Fig. No. 12 and Plate No. 30.) These tanks are each supplied with a vent pipe, which is carried up to the side of the ship for allowing air to enter the tank when petrol is drawn therefrom. The tanks on frames 6 and 7 are connected to a supply tank in the foremost gondola; the other tanks are connected to a supply tank in the after gondola. When petrol is required it is run from the tanks on the transverse frame into the supply tank by merely turning on a cock, which is turned off when the supply tank is full. This can only be done when the ship is on an even keel. There is a cross-connection between the petrol supply tanks for the forward gondola and those for the after gondola, which enables the whole of the supply to be used in one car if necessary. In the cars the petrol flows from the supply tank to the petrol pump of the engine, from where it is pumped to the carburettor by a mechanical piston pump incorporated in the design of the engine. (Figs. 13 and 14.)

Propellers.

The forward engine drives two swivelling propellers. These propellers were manufactured by the Integral Propeller Company, Hendon. They are four-bladed, 12 ft. diameter, and made up of nine laminations at the boss.

The single propeller of the after engine was manufactured by the Farringdon Engineering Company. It is a two-bladed propeller of 17 ft. diameter. The material is the best Honduras mahogany, the laminations being $\frac{7}{8}$ in. thick. As a finish the wood is varnished only. The thickness at the boss is $9\frac{5}{8}$ ins. (Plate No. 31.)

Fire Preventions.

Pyrene extinguishers are provided to deal with an outbreak of fire should one occur. Four are carried in each engine room and three in each navigating compartment, making a total of seven for each car.

They are also placed at frequent intervals throughout the keel walking-way of the ship.

The following three orders, as precautionary measures against fire, are embodied in the standing engine-room orders :—

1. Any leakage of petrol is to be immediately wiped up, and the defect repaired.
2. No oily waste is to be left about.
3. Petrol is not to be used for cleaning purposes.

The following are general rules to be observed in case of fire :—

If fire should break out in either gondola the petrol supply to that gondola to be turned off.

The other gondola not to stop engines, unless fire spreads to the fabric of the keel cover.

The way of the ship to be stopped and the ship to be landed as soon as possible.

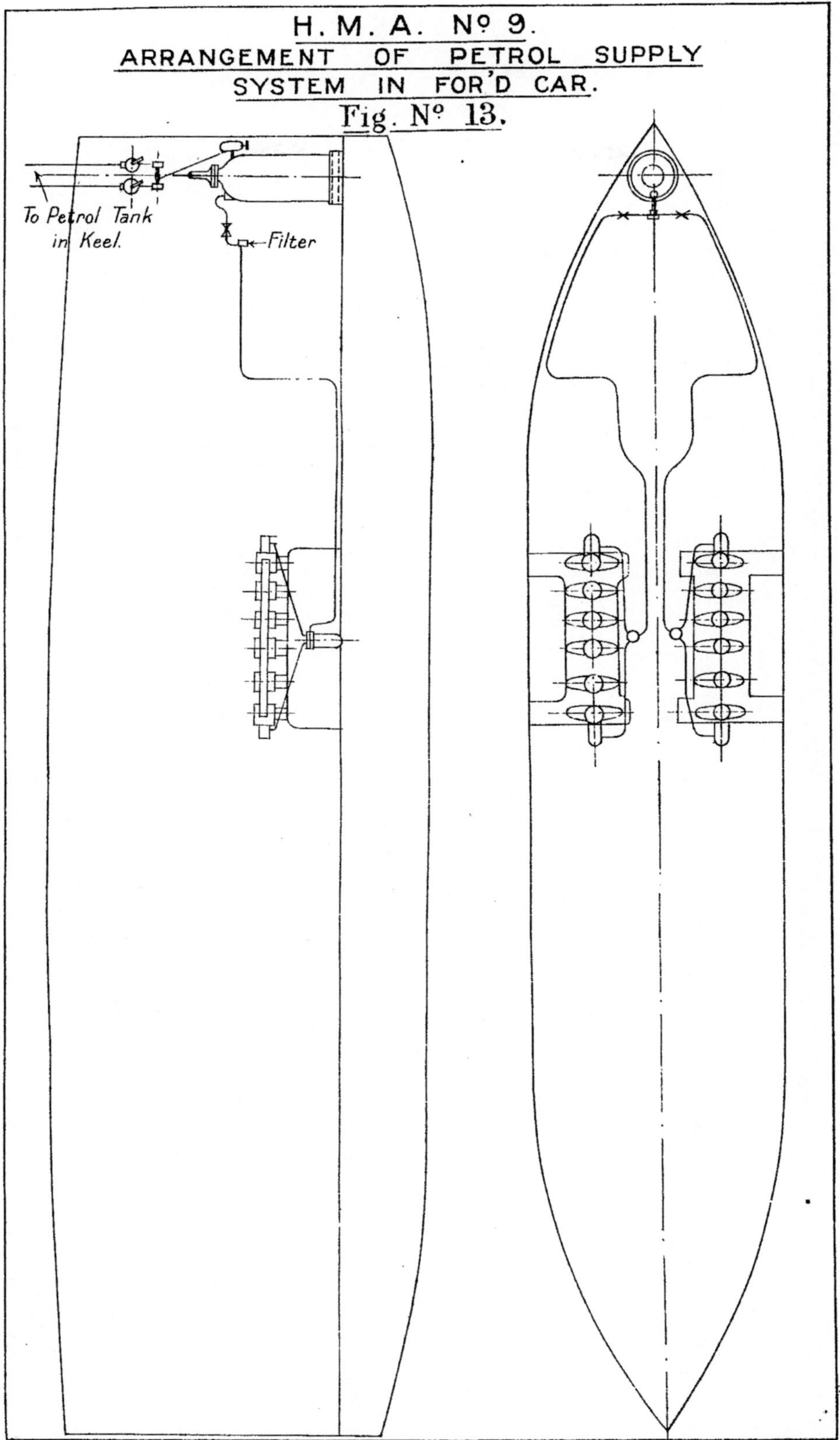

727/.

Malby & Sons, Lith.

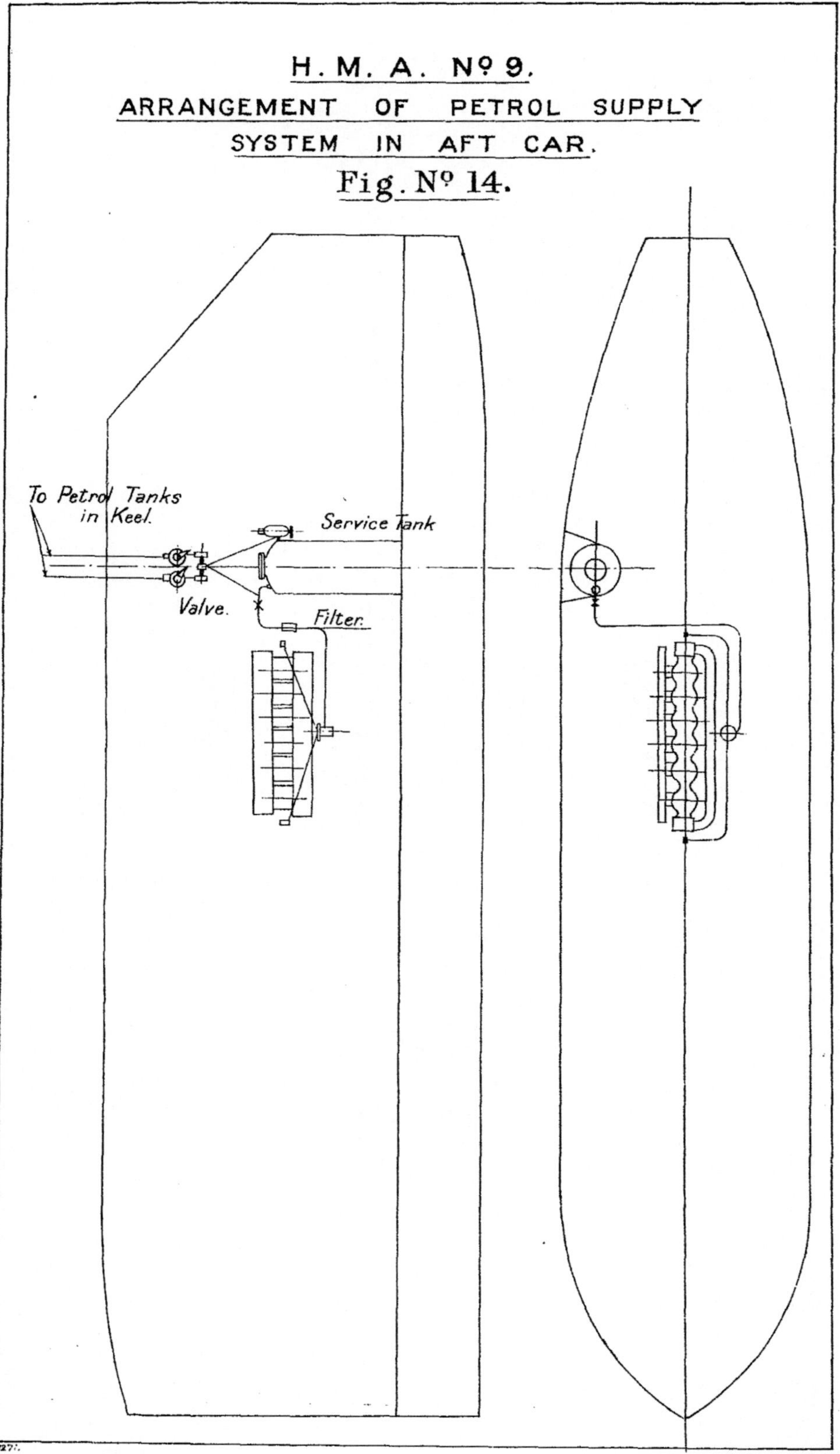

H. M. A. Nº 9.
ARRANGEMENT OF PETROL SUPPLY SYSTEM IN AFT CAR.
Fig. Nº 14.

Malby & Sons, Lith.

To face p. 30.

Plate No. 30. Petrol Tank with Fittings.

AS 4751

Plate No. 31. Single Propeller in After Car.

To face p. 31.

PLATE NO. 32.
AFTER CAR, SHOWING STEERING WHEEL AND PEDESTAL, INSTRUMENTS, ETC.

CHAPTER V.

Instruments and Navigation Appliances—Controls—Ballast and Ballast Discharge—Mooring and Handling Arrangements.

Instruments and Navigation Appliances.

Instruments are disposed in the ship as follows :—

Gun Platform.

1 standard compass fitted to bracket on top tail of gun platform.

Forward Car.

1 back bearing compass (Pattern 254).
1 steering compass, A.V. type, fitted with binnacle.
1 bubble statoscope.
1 Short and Mason statoscope.
1 Ogilvie speed indicator.
3 aneroids.
2 inclinometers.
1 eight-day clock.
2 Elliott speed indicators (one for each engine).
1 engine-room telegraph to forward engine room.
1 engine-room telegraph to after engine room.

After Car. (Plate No. 32.)

1 steering compass, A.V. type, fitted with binnacle.
1 aneroid.
1 statoscope.
1 eight-day clock.
1 speed indicator, belonging to the German Maybach engine.
1 engine-room telegraph to after engine room.
1 engine-room telegraph to forward engine room.

Controls.

Valve Controls.—All the hand-controlled valves are controlled from the foremost gondola. The valve ropes are attached to steel wire strands ·07 in. diameter at the top members of the keel. The steel wire passes through a guide pulley attached at the apex of the keel, and runs along the same level to the next section of keel, when it is transferred to another pulley at the top of the keel. It is kept in position at the bottom by a wire running to an attachment on the bottom tube.

It will be seen from the diagram how the pull on the control causes the downward pull on the valve cord until the maximum valve opening of 3½ ins. is reached. (Fig. No. 15.)

After passing through the top pulley the wire controls run through guides along the top member of the keel until the forward gondola is reached.

Elevator and Rudder Controls.—The elevators and rudders are under dual control from the forward and after cars. When the ship is in flight they are controlled from the forward car, but, should any breakdown occur in the wires, they can be disconnected and coupled up to the control of the after car.

The rudder wheel is situated at the forward end of the car beneath the compass, and the elevator wheel on the starboard side of the car. Each can be thrown out of gear. The handwheel, by means of a spur wheel, drives the chain wheel. To the chains are attached the wire controls which are carried along the keel of the ship beyond the after car. These pass through a fixed and sliding pulley to two gear wheels and from thence to the stern post of the ship, and through guide pulleys to the elevators and rudders themselves. (Plates 33 and 34.) An indicator shows, in degrees, the angles of elevation or depression of the elevators.

The rudder controls were found to work stiffly during the trial flight. To overcome this a reduction gear box was fitted and the arrangement of the controls became as shown in Fig. No. 16.

The maximum angle of rudders and elevators is 25°. The maximum turns of wheel to produce full helm is 11, that is, from midships to hard over.

Ballast and Ballast Discharge.—As the ship was originally designed, water ballast was to be carried in three tanks similar to the petrol tanks and of a capacity of 130 gallons, situated at transverse frames Nos. 3, 9, and 14. In addition there were to have been four fabric ballast bags, but these were never fitted.

The tanks discharge through a rubbered canvas hose which passes through the keel of the ship. At the bottom of the hose is fitted a valve with an arm to which the control wire is attached. This passes over a pulley at the top of the keel and leads to the forward car. All ballast controls are worked from the forward gondola.

Mooring and Handling Arrangements.

The mooring and hauling-down ropes are carried while the ship is in flight in boxes in the keel and are attached to the foot of the keel. The side handling guys are attached to the top members of the keel on each side.

At Frame 3.—Forward hauling-down rope, Manilla hemp, 3½ in. circumference (breaking load 7·5 tons), length 300 feet.

Sea anchor rope and hauling-down wire rope—1¼-in. circumference (B.L. 7·5 tons), length 300 ft.

H.

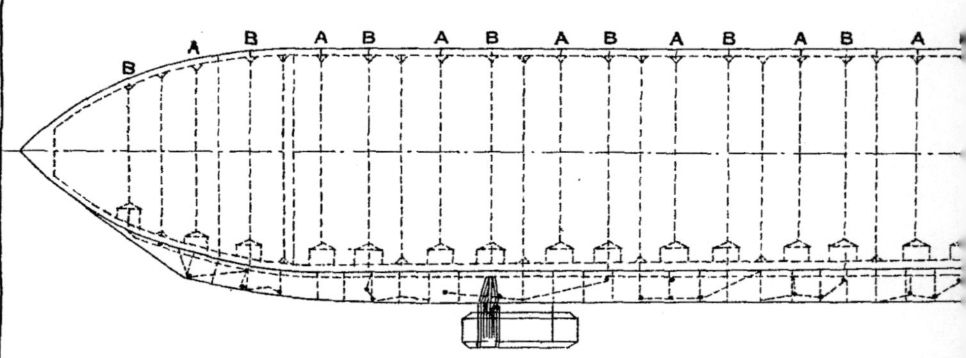

ELEVATION

A. AUTOMATIC RELEASE

B. AUTOMATIC & HAND C

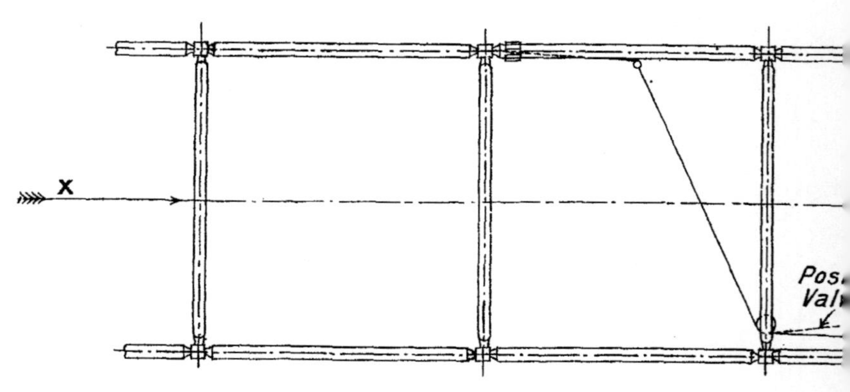

ARRANGEMENT

GAS VALVE CON

Nº 9.

15.

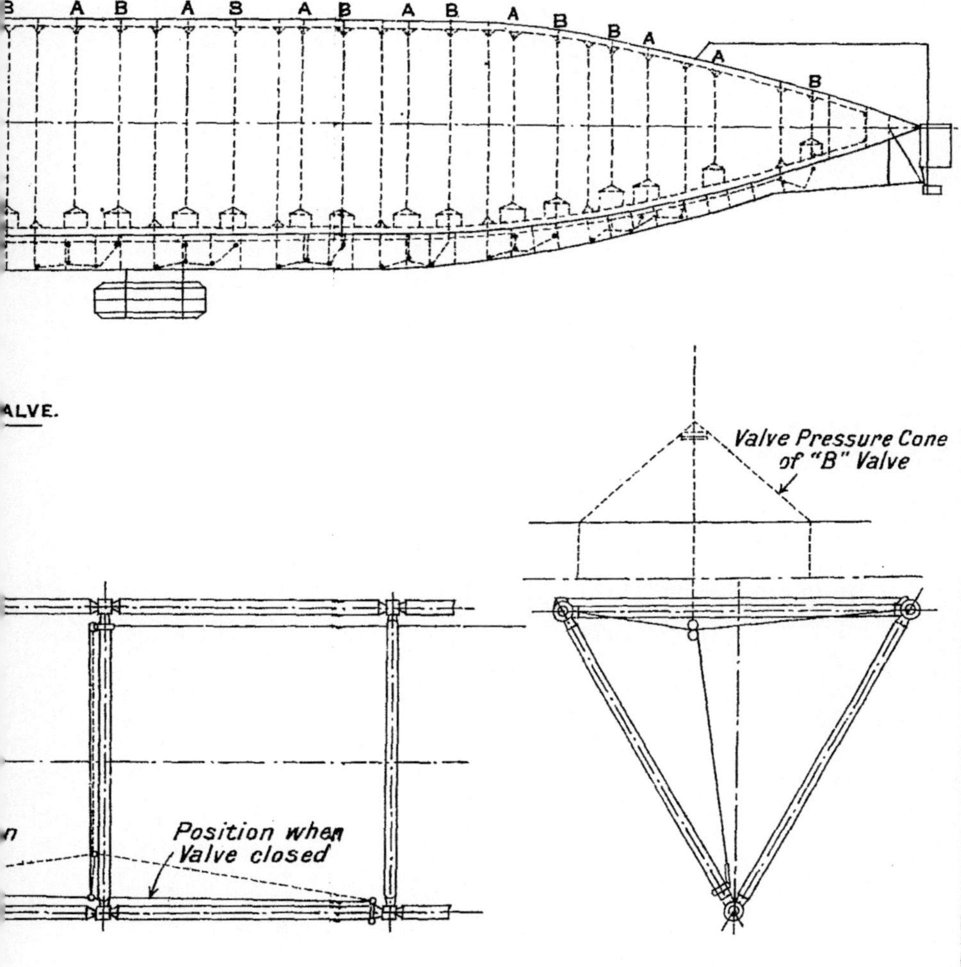

END VIEW.

LOOKING IN DIRECTION OF ARROW "X"

Malby & Sons, Lith.

H. M. A. Nº9.

DIAGRAMMATIC ARRANGEMENT OF CONTROLS.

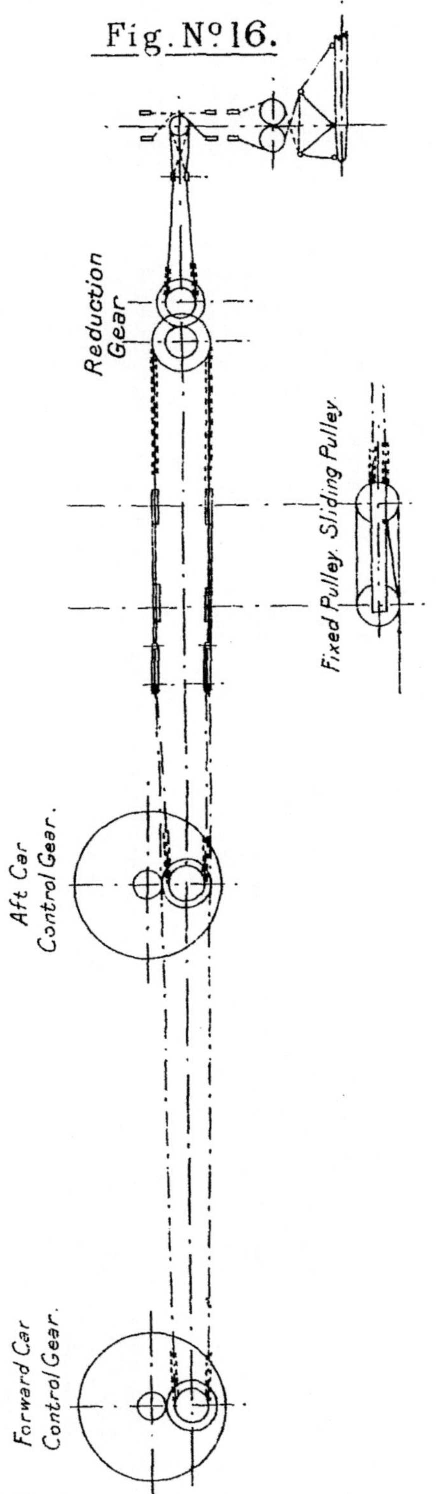

7271.
Malby & Sons, Lith.

To face p. 32.

PLATE NO. 33.

ELEVATORS AND RUDDERS, SHOWING COTROL WIRES.

To face p. 33.

PLATE NO. 34.
ELEVATORS AND RUDDERS, SHOWING CONTROL WIRES.

Main mooring rope, Cradocks' wire, 2½ in. circumference (B.L. 20 tons). This is fitted with a spring buffer gear in a tube beneath the bottom tube of the keel; length, 55 ft.

Two side guys, Cradocks' wire rope, ¾ in. circumference (B.L. 2 tons); length, 60 ft.

At Frame 2.—Two side guys, Cradocks' wire rope, ¾ in. circumference (B.L. 2 tons); length, 60 ft.

At Frames 7, 8, 9, *and* 12.—Two side guys, Cradocks' wire rope, ¾ in. circumference (B.L. 2 tons); length, 20 ft.

At Frames 13, 15, 16, *and* 17.—Two side guys, Cradocks' wire rope, ¾ in. circumference (B.L. 2 tons); length, 60 ft.

At Frame 14.—After hauling-down rope, 2½ in. circumference; Italian hemp (B.L. 2·4 tons); length, 150 ft.

Side handling ropes for all side guys consist of three pieces of hemp 2½ in. circumference (B.L. 2·4 tons), three holding grips fitted to each, attached to guys with a toggle; length, 30 ft.

All side guys are fitted with toggle eyes at the ends for attaching handling ropes.

The side guys at frames 2, 3, 16, and 17 have also ¾-in. steel wire toggle eyes which are spliced to the guys at the same height above ground as the ends of the short guys. The handling ropes can be attached to these for convenience in handling the ship in the shed. The last six feet of the long guys are covered with leather. The guys are attached to the keel by a screw shackle passing through a lug on the junction piece into which the longitudinal tubes of the keel fit.

The trail ropes are secured to the bottom member of the keel by a strop which passes over the junction piece and is secured underneath by a shackle with a bolt and nut.

The trail ropes are carried in a box fitting in the apex of the keel. The door of the box is hinged at the bottom and is released by a spring bar controlled from the car. The rope, which has been resting on the door, automatically falls out when the door drops. The forward trail rope is controlled in the forward gondola and the after trail rope in the after car.

The sea anchor rope is connected to a canvas drogue of a capacity of 166 cubic feet. The rope passes over a drum fitted at the bottom of the keel and leads from this to a small winch which is situated fore and aft in the keel.

Handling Party.

The handling party is disposed as follows :—

Handling Officer.—Generally in charge of ship whilst on the ground.

Stern Handling Officer.—In charge of the stern.

Bow Handling Officer.—In charge of the bow.

Handling C.P.O.—In charge of handling party and to assist stern officer when actually moving ship.

Assistant C.P.O.—Assists handling C.P.O. and bow officer when actually moving ship.

Second Assistant C.P.O.—In charge of gondola party and hauling-down rope.

It has been shown that there are 10 guys each side, with three tails to a guy.

Nos. 1 and 2 guys are known as the fore guys.
Nos. 3, 4, 5, 6, and 7 are known as the midship guys.
Nos. 8, 9, and 10 are known as the after guys.

A P.O. or L.M. is detailed to take charge of each of the fore, midship, and after guys.

Each guy is under the charge of a rating termed "the leading hand of the guy," who is responsible for the toggling and untoggling and that orders given with reference to his guy are obeyed.

Hands are detailed to each guy and a party for each gondola. On the order "Man the guys" the guy and gondola parties immediately move off direct to their proper stations. Each man has his appointed station and should be thoroughly acquainted with the position he has to take up.

The hands on the guys are divided into permanent guy hands and reinforcing guy hands. The permanent guy hands always remain on their guys.

To reinforce starboard guys if required, No. 1 guy port reinforces No. 1 starboard, and so on; and also vice versa.

To reinforce foremost or after guys Nos. 4, 5, 6, and 7 are used.

No. 4 guy reinforces No. 1 guy.
No. 5 guy reinforces No. 2 guy.
No. 6 guy reinforces No. 9 guy.
No. 7 guy reinforces No. 10 guy.

For landing ship, the permanent guy hands place themselves under their respective wire pendants, remaining there to toggle on when the order is given. Gondola parties place themselves under their respective gondolas. Nos. 3, 4, 5, 6, and 7 guys (less permanent guy hands) form the foremost hauling-down party. Two hands from the foremost gondola are responsible for snatching the foremost hauling-down rope, after which they man the stopper. When the hauling-down rope is slipped and made up, they stand by the mooring rope, if used.

The after hauling-down rope, if required, is manned by Nos. 8 and 9 guys (less permanent guy hands).

This routine holds good at all times for the handling party; of course, the force of the wind will determine the number of hands required, and other circumstances the action to be taken to meet eventualities.

To face p. 34.

PLATE NO. 35.
H.M.A. NO. 9 MOORED OUT.

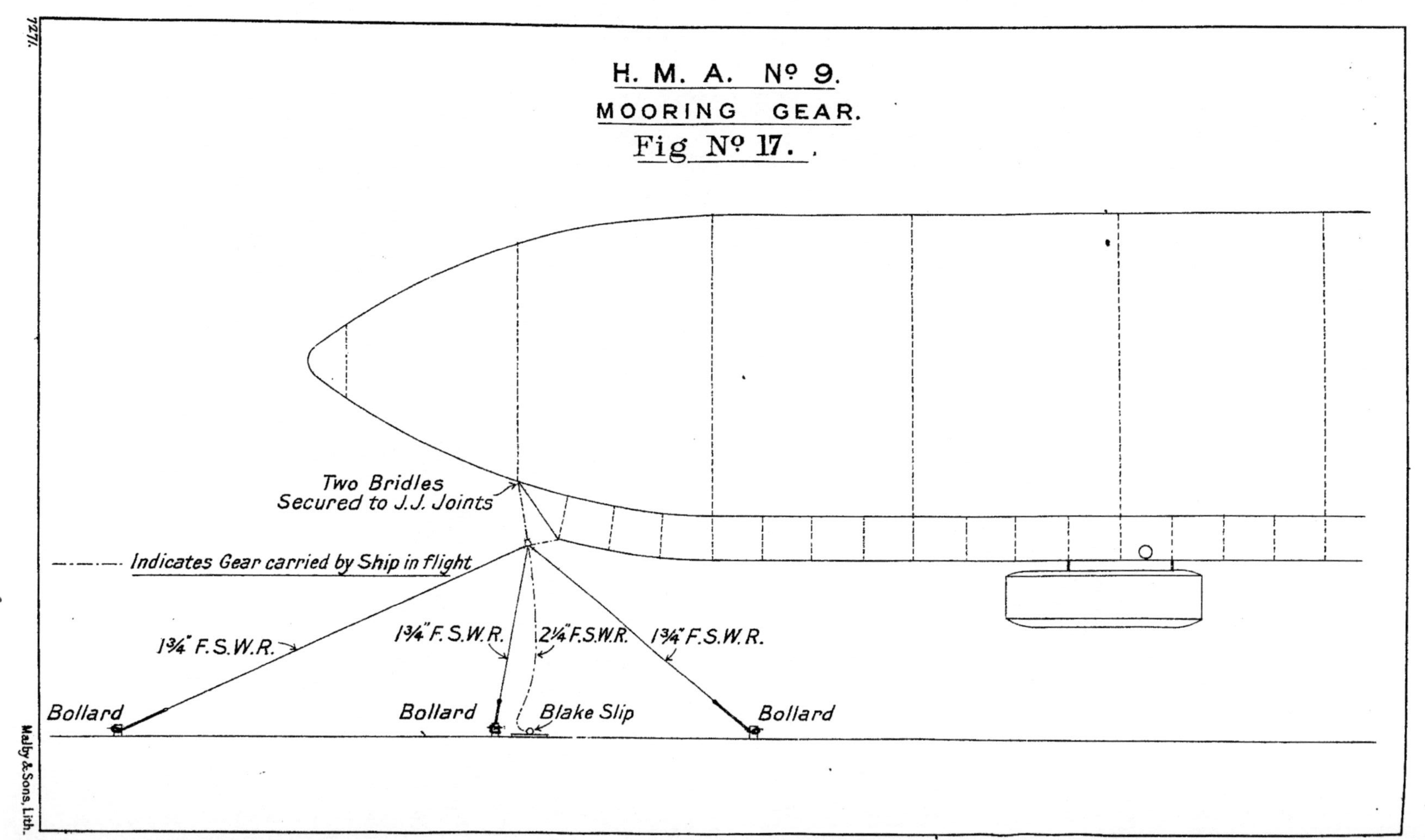
H. M. A. Nº 9.
MOORING GEAR.
Fig Nº 17.
Two Bridles
Secured to J.J. Joints
Indicates Gear carried by Ship in flight
1¾" F.S.W.R.
1¾" F.S.W.R.
2¼" F.S.W.R.
1¾" F.S.W.R.
Bollard
Bollard
Blake Slip
Bollard
7271.
Malby & Sons, Lith.

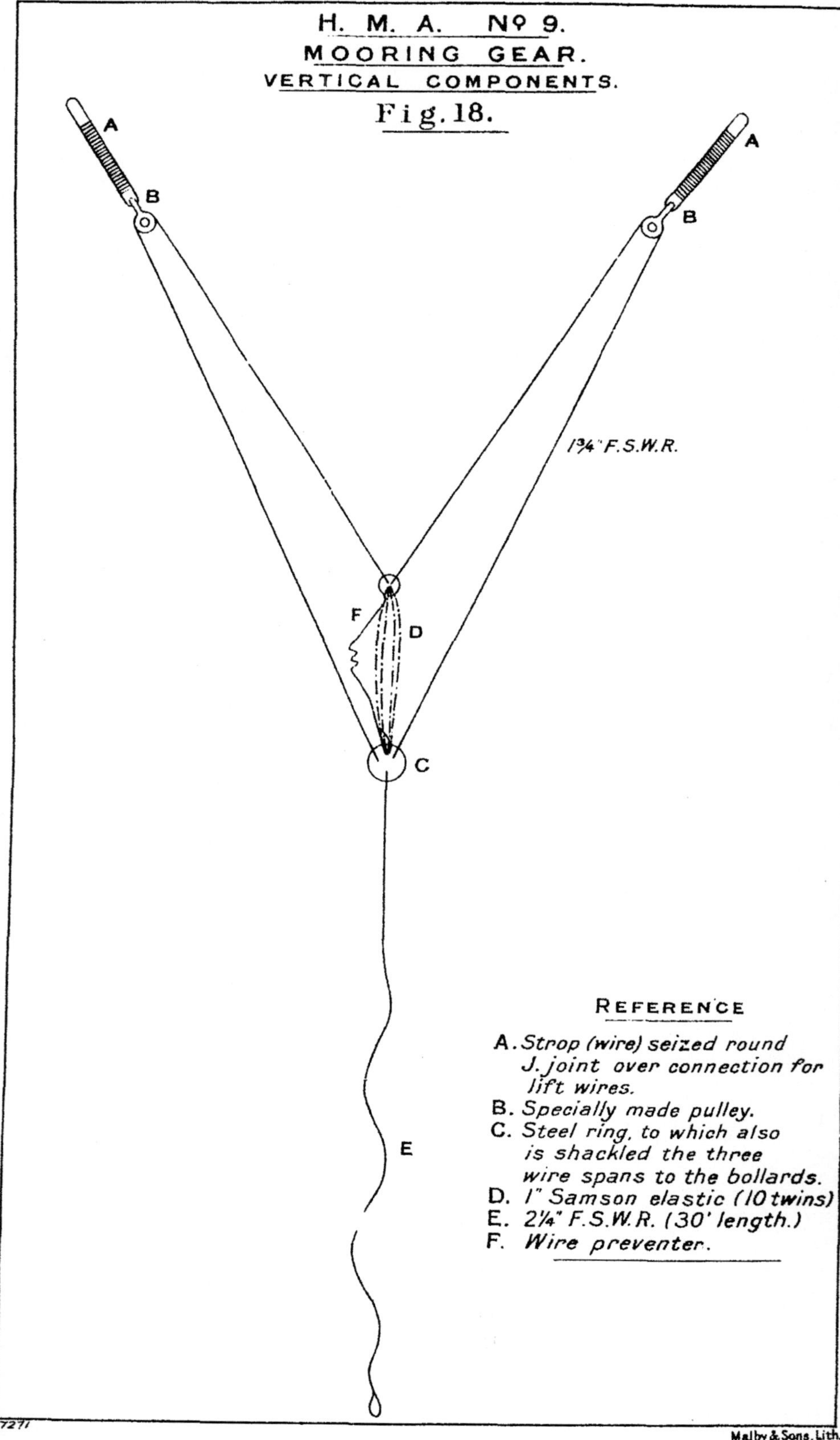
H. M. A. Nº 9.
MOORING GEAR.
VERTICAL COMPONENTS.
Fig. 18.
A
B
A
B
1¾" F.S.W.R.
F
D
C
E
REFERENCE
A. Strop (wire) seized round J. joint over connection for lift wires.
B. Specially made pulley.
C. Steel ring, to which also is shackled the three wire spans to the bollards.
D. 1" Samson elastic (10 twins)
E. 2¼" F.S.W.R. (30' length.)
F. Wire preventer.
7271
Malby & Sons, Lith.

Mooring Out.

Figure No. 17 shows the method of triangulation.

The three bollards round the mooring ring are each 60 ft. from the mooring ring.

Three wire spans, 60 ft. long, of $1\frac{3}{4}$-in. F.S.W.R., and each having a 4-in. hemp tail, 10 ft. long spliced in the end, are shackled at their upper ends by means of a 5-ton shackle into a steel ring which also carries the three legs which lead respectively to the two J.J. and the foremost points of the keel.

The actual method used for giving the mooring gear a certain amount of elasticity is shown on the accompanying sketch. (Fig. No. 18.)

The $2\frac{1}{4}$-in. wire attached to the mooring ring by a slip is merely used as a " preventer " in case one of the other spans carries away.

To secure to the moorings.—The ship is walked over the mooring ring, and the $2\frac{1}{4}$-in. wire is fastened to the slip. The three wire spans are then shackled on to the ring attached to the ship.

Toggle-ropes carrying $\frac{1}{2}$-cwt. sinkers, about six in number to each car, are made fast to the handling rails of the cars. These ropes vary in length so that they touch the ground in succession as the ship comes down. The longest is about 15 ft. in length.

The ship is then let up about 500 lbs. light to a height of about 30 ft., *i.e.*, distance of fore part of keel from the ground, in such a way that the mooring point is vertically above the centre of the triangle formed by the three bollards round the mooring ring. The three legs are then made fast round the bollards.

No. 9 rides best carrying a little " up " helm, which ensures the bow being kept up and the mooring spans kept taut.

Gassing Ship.—On one occasion the foremost six gasbags were gassed from tubes which were carried on a lorry. A fabric main, stretching the full length of the ship with connections to each gasbag, has been made, and will be used for gassing when moored out. This main will be laid along the keel inside the ship, and connection made to the gas main at the mooring ring. (This method was not used on the occasion mentioned.)

Petrol is taken in from cans.

Ballast.—Water-ballast is taken in from wheeled tanks, although it would be difficult to do this if the wind was changeable, especially to fill the after tank.

Handling Party.—About 80 men are required :—

15 men on each fore guy (60).

10 men on each car (20).

The men on the guys simply help to check any tendency of the bow to move off the wind.

Those on the cars stand by to catch them if there is any tendency to bump.

The men on the after car sometimes have to put their weight on to prevent the stern going up too high. These men haul on the toggle-ropes that hold the sinkers.

One watch, *i.e.*, two officers, three seamen, one W/T operator and two engineers, only remain in the ship when moored out. One helmsman is kept at the wheel and one engineer in each engine room, the remainder of the watch being moved about as necessary for trimming ship. The occasions on which No. 9 has moored out are as follows :—

Date.	Time moored out.	Maximum Wind experienced.	Weather Conditions.	Remarks.
1. 26.5.17	11 hours	28 knots	bc	Triangulation tried for the first time. Refuelled from petrol cans.
2. 20.6.17	2 hours	15 knots	bcr	Rain leaked through the outer cover and down the wiring to the keel and cars. Gas valves were filled with water.
3. 2.7.17	14¼ hours	24 knots	bc	Wind very changeable, varying 6 points. Damaged bows while unmooring.
4. 13.8.17	4 hours	18 knots	bcq	Gassed ship. Nos. 1–6 bags. Refuelled with petrol cans.
5. 29.10.17	2 hours	27 knots	oc	

CHAPTER VI.

Wireless Telegraphy—Armament—Electric Lighting—Telephones, etc.

W/T Apparatus.

The wireless cabin is fitted with a main transmitter, an auxiliary transmitter, receiver, and the necessary aerial for radiating and receiving. (Plate No. 36.)

The Main Transmitter.

The main transmitter is type 56 and generates continuous waves. This instrument is made by the Marconi Co., and is suitable for ranges up to 350–400 miles. The energy used is of the order of 30 watts and is obtained from a 1,000-volt dry battery. It is proposed to fit a stand-by battery which can be brought into action by change-over plugs or switch. The current taken by the valve filament is 4·5 amperes and is supplied from a six-volt battery. Two other units are supplied with this transmitter—a switch for breaking the high-tension circuit, and a key unit, which contains a "trigger" battery, consisting of 18 dry cells.

To face p. 36.

PLATE No. 36.

WIRELESS SET.

To face p. 37.

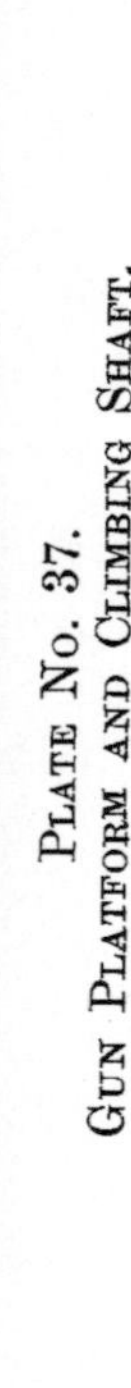

Plate No. 37.
Gun Platform and Climbing Shaft.

The Auxiliary Transmitter.

The auxiliary transmitter is a type 52 modified, which is worked from an eight-volt battery. A double-pole change-over switch transfers the aerial and earth from the main to the auxiliary transmitter or vice versa.

The Receiver.

The receiver is a model Tc, which is suitable for the reception of spark signals up to a wave-length of approximately 600 metres. For the reception of weak signals a model Tb relay (Triple valve amplifier) is used in conjunction with the above receiver. A combined receiver and amplifier will shortly be fitted in lieu of the Tc receiver and Tb relay. This receiver (model Tf) can be used for the reception of either spark or continuous waves, and will enable airships to intercommunicate between themselves or with their bases with a minimum risk of interference.

The Aerial.

The aerial is carried on a reel mounted on the starboard side of the operating table and consists of 300 ft. of wire. Attached to the end is a streamline weight of lead of about 4 lbs. An ebonite deck insulator is fitted directly below the aerial reel, and projects about 12 inches below the deck. A spare aerial is carried in case the other should be carried away. A hand-hole trap-door is fitted alongside the deck insulator to facilitate the shipping of a new aerial and weight.

Communication with other parts of the ship is established by a loud-speaking telephone fitted to the after bulkhead.

An Aldis lamp is carried for visual signalling, and a cupboard is fitted for the stowage of code books, tools, and the necessary spares. An aneroid, 8-day watch, and C.W. wavemeter complete the outfit. On the port side of the keel, outside the W/T cabin, a flag locker is fitted.

The total weight of all W/T instruments, including one H.T. battery and aerial, is 220 lbs.

Armament.

This had to be cut down to the lowest degree possible, on account of the lack of lift. When the ship was first stationed at Howden she carried only two Lewis guns and three bombs.

One Lewis gun was mounted on the gun platform on the top of the hull at No. 3 transverse frame. This platform, which is built up of duralumin sections, is 4 ft. 6 in. diameter over all, and is circular in shape. It is approached by a climbing tube which is adjacent to No. 3 frame, and the adjoining gasbag is slightly hollowed to give the necessary room. (Plate No. 36.)

The second Lewis gun was carried in the after car, and was mounted on a pedestal fitted to the outside of the car at the bottom level of the window next to the engine-room bulkhead.

The three 100-lb. bombs were fitted to frames attached to the handling rail of the after car. Two were carried on the port and one on the starboard side. They were released by the ordinary Bowden wire release gear.

Electric Lighting.

A somewhat extensive scheme of lighting was originally proposed, with the power to be generated by a 2-k.w. dynamo driven off one of the after engines. The dynamo in itself was considered to be too heavy when the general cutting down of weight was found imperative, and the great amount of light in the cars rendered it impossible to see anything at all outside. Lights sufficient for the working of the ship only are now provided.

Accumulators are fitted in both forward and after cars, and the following 12-volt lamps are fixed in each gondola, with the exception of the one over the chart table; which appears in the forward car only :—

1 for compass.
1 for indicator for rudders.
1 for indicator for elevators.
1 for each telegraph.
1 over chart table.
3 in engine room below roof.

In addition to these, there is a light in the W/T cabin, and the white recognition light in the keel of the ship abaft the forward car.

Telephones.

Telephonic communication is provided between the forward gondola and after gondola, from the forward gondola to the wireless cabin, and from the after gondola to the wireless cabin.

They are run off a 12-volt accumulator. The instruments are fitted with a double receiver, which is heavily padded with india-rubber to render it sound-proof.

In the event of the telephone bells not being heard in the engine rooms Klaxon horns are fitted, the calls being from forward car to forward engine room, forward car to after engine room, and after car to after engine room.

A 12-volt battery in each gondola supplies the power, the cable being 1/18 cab-tyre sheathed.

CHAPTER VII.

Log of Construction—Tests and Trials carried out during Construction—Method of Inflation.

Engine Trials.

During the latter half of the month of August 1916 the machinery installations in both the cars of the ships were on the verge of completion, and arrangements were made for various trials to be carried out.

On August 28th one hour's full power trial of the forward installation was carried out, and on the whole, the results were satisfactory. No perceptible vibration was noticed and the running of the gearing appeared satisfactory. It was decided after consideration to carry out some slight modifications to the lubricating system.

On September 9th an attempt was made to carry out a six hours' trial of the machinery in the forward car. Owing to a large leakage of oil from the propeller gear boxes to the swivelling arms this trial had to be abandoned. The installation was run for two hours so that experience might be gained, and it was decided that the lubricating arrangements should be further modified.

On September 17th, alterations having been effected, the six hours' trial previously attempted was carried out. The engines ran satisfactorily, but, on inspection after the trial, perceptible wear was noticed on the bevel wheels of the transmission gears. It was also decided that, as the silencers which had been fitted were not satisfactory, new ones of the Zeppelin type should be constructed.

On September 22nd a one hour's trial of the machinery of the after car was held to test the gears, which were found to be bad, especially the propeller driving wheels. These wheels were refitted and stiffening bolts were added to the propeller boxes.

On September 27th the one hour's final shed trial of the engines of the forward gondola was held. On opening up, the gears were considered to be sufficiently satisfactory for the flight trials to be carried out without any radical alterations to the existing arrangements.

During the month of October the ship was inflated, and during this period the engines were overhauled and run for short periods on several occasions, to gain as much efficiency as possible for the two hours' air-borne trial required before the trial flights.

On November 12th the two hours' air-borne machinery trial was carried out, and the results were quite satisfactory.

This completes the enumeration of the trials as carried out before the ship was completed and ready for the trial flights. Several trials were held after these flights, but, as they were consequent on the change of power units decided upon later, they will be dealt with in the next chapter, which includes, in addition to the description of the flights themselves, the alterations and the trials involved after the initial flights.

Inflation and Lift Trials.

It is now considered opportune briefly to describe the inflation and lift trials of the ship. It must be borne in mind that the difficulties experienced were almost entirely due to a lack of disposable lift, and to overcome this the majority of the gasbags were changed on two occasions.

Arrangements for Inflation.

Three thousand tubes were stacked and the hydrogen-filling arrangements tested.

The main having been tested and modifications arranged for, the pressures and purities of the tubes were taken.

Every tube was tapped in the female connection, in order that there might be no difficulty in screwing in the flexible connections. As a further precaution against delays, each iron cap was removed, and, if too tight, was eased before being screwed on again.

The filling parties were drilled in connecting up and disconnecting, and were given instructions in case of fire. It is noteworthy that, while the average time for connecting up 10 bottles and connecting the filler to the branch pipe was, at the beginning of the drill, 1½ minutes, it was reduced by drill to about 50 seconds.

Precautionary Measures for the Inflation.

Besides the usual precautions of fire parties, chemical extinguishers, &c., the following devices were fitted :—

Gastight telephone from control position in the shed to control position in the hydrogen stowage (Plate No. 38), enabling direct and continuous communication between the officer in charge of inflation and the officer in charge of stowage.

Electric bell in the fire pump room, operated by gastight switches—one situated at the inflation control station and one at the hydrogen stowage station.

Electric bell at the master valve, operated by gastight switches—one situated in the main shed and one in the hydrogen stowage.

Electric bell at the control position in the hydrogen stowage, operated by gastight switch at the water seal.

The above system of telephone and electrical signals enabled :—

Continuous communication between the inflation control position and the hydrogen stowage control.

Signal to be sent from either control position in case of emergency, for the closing of the master valve.

Signal to be sent in case of emergency from either control position for the starting of the fire pump.

Signal to be sent from the water seal to the hydrogen control position in the event of the water seal being blown.

Arrangements in the Hydrogen Stowage.

The arrangements in the hydrogen stowage were as follows :—

A control position was built, enabling the officer in charge of the stowage to overlook the complete stowage. At this position the telephone and various electrical signalling devices already described were fitted up, together with a water U tube showing the pressure in the main.

Personnel.—To each 10-way filler four hands were told off—one the leading hand in charge of the standpipe valve, the re-

To face p. 40.

PLATE NO. 38.

CONTROL POSITION, HYDROGEN STOWAGE.

To face p. 40.

PLATE NO. 39. BAGS IN SHIP READY FOR INFLATION.

To face p. 41.

PLATE No. 40. GASBAGS INFLATED 20 PER CENT.

maining three for connecting up the flexible hoses and turning on and off the cylinder valves.

The connections being made to the cylinders, the assistant officer in charge of the stowage inspected each party's connections and reported them to the officer in charge of the stowage, prior to any order being given for turning on.

The parties were divided into two portions—port and starboard, five parties being placed on the port side of the stowage and five on the starboard side. These groups discharged alternately. While the starboard parties were discharging, the port parties would be reconnecting up and marking up the last used tubes as empty, tying the necessary labels, &c.

The actual speeds of inflation, which are indicated in detail in the attached log, were :—

5th October.—300 tubes discharged in 63 minutes, *i.e.*, at the rate of 107,000 cubic feet per hour.

6th October.—650 tubes discharged in 1 hour 57 minutes, *i.e.*, at the rate of 117,000 cubic feet per hour.

6th October.—500 tubes discharged in 70 minutes, *i.e.*, at the rate of 161,000 cubic feet per hour.

11th October.—550 tubes discharged in 66 minutes, *i.e.* at the rate of 187,500 cubic feet per hour.

11th October.—150 tubes discharged in 17 minutes, *i.e.*, at the rate of 198,500 cubic feet per hour.

Subsequent discharge of tubes was entirely for filling up individual bags and testing valves.

Plates Nos. 39 and 40 show the inflation of the ship at various stages.

Inflation and Lift Trials.

Inflation was commenced on October 5th. It was decided to fill the ship to between 55 per cent. to 60 per cent. full, and then fit the outer cover. No difficulty was encountered, the bags went into place easily and appeared to fit well. The outer cover was then fitted, but not laced. The inflation was then continued until the ship was from 92 per cent. to 95 per cent. full. The adjustment of the valves was then carried out in sequence from each end, each bag being fully inflated in turn.

The purity of the various bags at the end of inflation was as follows :—

No. 1—95·75 per cent.
No. 2—96·92 per cent.
No. 3—96·39 per cent.
No. 4—96·39 per cent.
No. 5—96·45 per cent.
No. 6—96·86 per cent.
No. 7—97·33 per cent.
No. 8—96·92 per cent.
No. 9—94·52 per cent.
No. 10—96·92 per cent.
No. 11—96·17 per cent.
No. 12—96·86 per cent.
No. 13—97·06 per cent.
No. 14—96·59 per cent.
No. 15—97·26 per cent.
No. 16—96·72 per cent.
No. 17—93·91 per cent.

The testing and adjusting of the gasbag valves was commenced with No. 2 bag. On the first test, after the adjustment of the lower cones, the valves blew off at 1·5 to 2 mm. pressure.

This was considered too low and the length of the valve cord was increased by lowering the cone. Pressure was again put in the bag, and on reaching 5 mm. something was heard to break. Pressure was at once reduced to zero. It was found that the transverse girders between A and B and B and C on the starboard side of No. 3 frame had buckled.

Similar tests were carried out in the parallel portion of the ship, No. 7 bag being selected. Nos. 6 and 8 bags were just filled and the pressure raised in No. 7 bag to 8 mm. Certain of the top transverse frames showed symptoms of buckling and the pressure was not raised further. The pressures in adjoining bags were—No. 6 bag, 1·5 mm.; No. 8 bag, 2 mm. It was proposed to stiffen the transverse girders with wood filling pieces. However, before fitting these it was considered practicable to slack off the chord wires in the adjoining frames. This was done, and No. 7 bag was raised to over 10 mm. pressure, and no damage was done. After this test the valve cords of No. 7 bag were so adjusted that the valve commenced to leak between 2 mm. and 3 mm. pressure.

Another test was taken of No. 10 bag with the chord wires removed, and, as the transverse girders appeared to stand perfectly satisfactorily, the wood filling to the transverse frames was abandoned and the chord wires were all disconnected.

The end loads at the transverse frames and the compressive forces applied to members of transverse frames in various conditions of contiguous gasbags are shown in the tables in Figs. Nos. 19 and 20. Fig. No. 21 illustrates the position of the gasbags at varying conditions of inflation.

On 23rd October the lift of the ship was measured. The lift per 1,000 cubic feet at 29·66 bar. and temperature 50° F. was 69·5 lbs., the total lift being 3·4 tons with the ship full.

As this did not satisfy contract requirements, Messrs. Vickers resolved to subject the whole ship to pressure, thereby stretching the bags. The following are the results of the pressure tests on Nos. 5, 6, and 7 bags :—

Object of Experiment.—To see if by putting up pressure of adjoining bags and leaving the pressure on for several hours, No. 6 bag could be induced to come further down.

Height.

4.30 p.m., 22nd October :—

No. 5.—2 mm., 3 ft. 9½ in; 8 mm., 2 ft. 5 in.

No. 6.—3 mm., 3 ft. 4½ in.; 11 mm., 2 ft. 6 in.

No. 7.—2 mm.,.3 ft. 10½ in.; 8 mm., 2 ft. 9¾ in.

8.30 a.m., 23rd October :—

No. 5.—6 mm., 2 ft. 5½ in.; 2 mm., 2 ft. 8½ in.

No. 6.—10 mm., 2 ft. 7 in.; 3 mm., 3 ft. 2¼ in.

No. 7.—6 mm., 2 ft. 10 in.; 2 mm., 3 ft. 1½ in.

Differences :—

No. 5.—1 ft. 1 in. down.

No. 6.—2¼ in. down.

No. 7.—9 in. down.

To face p. 42.

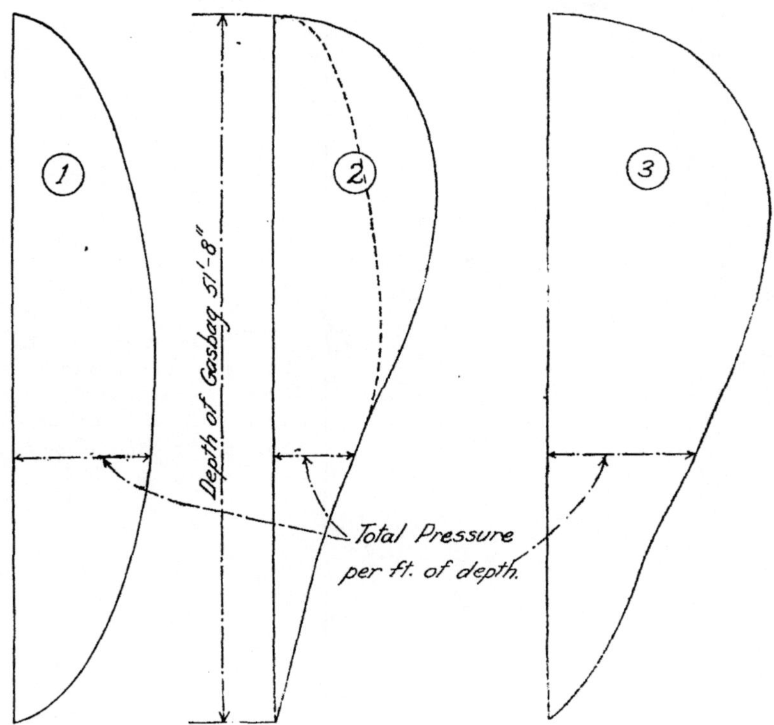

The following Table gives the conditions of contiguous bags (*a*) and (*b*) together with the total end loads for the three cases above:—

No.	Gasbag (*a*).	Gasbag (*b*).	Total End Load.
1	Normal 100 per cent. full	Super Press. 10 mm. -	4,280 lbs.
2	Deflated - - -	Normal, 100 per cent. full	3,550 ..
3	Deflated - - -	Super Press. 5 mm. -	5,690 ..

Fig. No. 19.

Diagram showing End Loads at Transverse Frames, with various conditions of Contiguous Gasbags.

a AS 4751

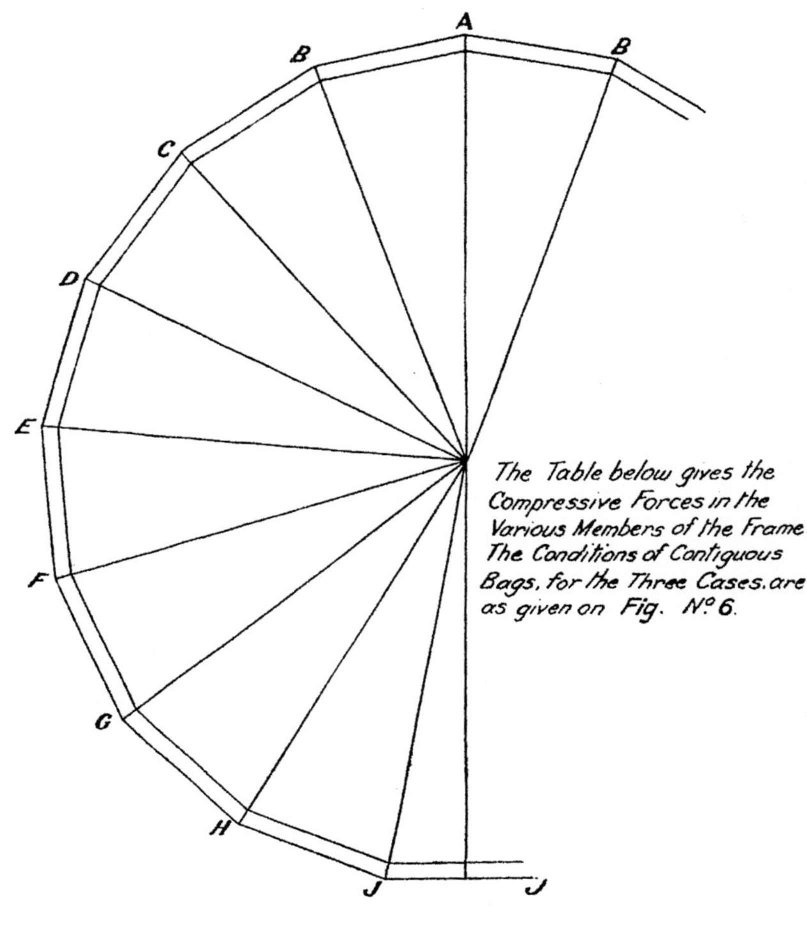

Member.	Force in Member.		
	1.	2.	3.
AB	2,330 lbs.	2,675 lbs.	3,365 lbs.
BC	2,480 „	2,780 „	3,405 „
CD	2,655 „	2,870 „	3,520 „
DE	2,915 „	2,960 „	3.640 „
EF	3,065 „	2,960 „	3,665 „
FG	3,175 „	2,960 „	3,660 „
GH	3,165 „	2,940 „	3,650 „
HJ	3,150 „	2,925 „	3,630 „
JJ	3,410 „	3,150 „	3,660 „

Fig. No. 20.

Diagram showing Forces in Members of a Transverse Frame

To face p. 42

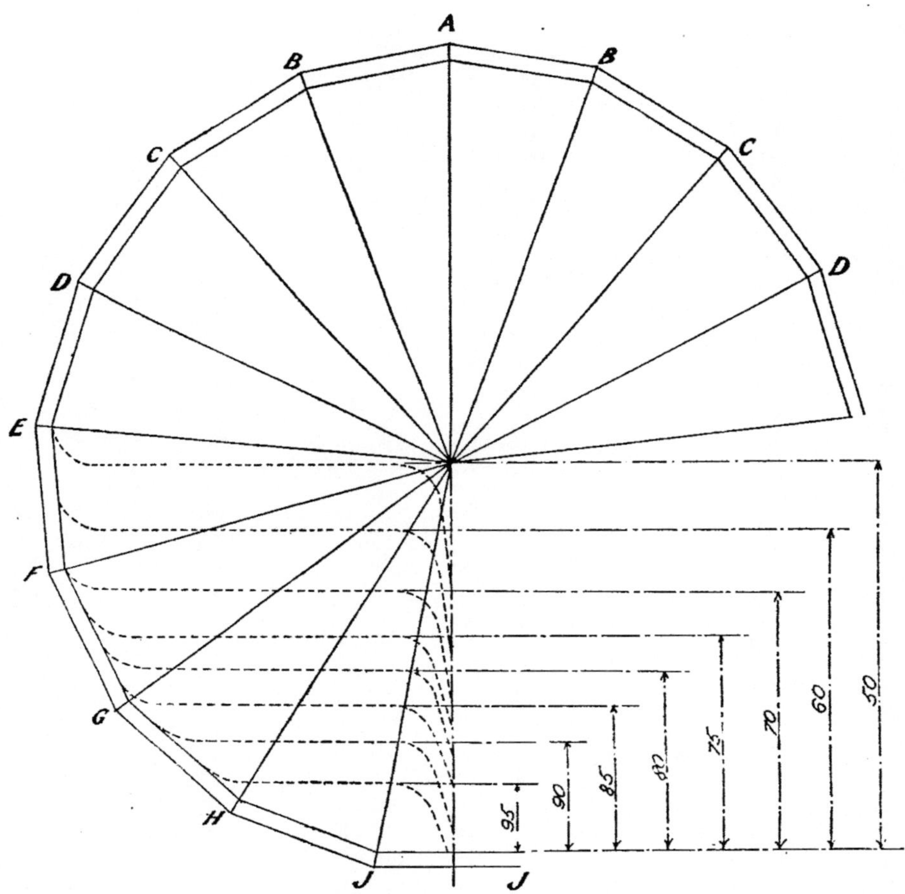

NOTE.—Lower surface of Gasbags is assumed approximate level.
Measurement made *from* inner side of J.J. Girders.

Percentage filled of Total Bag capacity. Per cent.	Approximate Height of Lower Surface of Bag. Ft. ins.
50	25 5
60	21 4
70	17 2
75	15 0
80	12 8
85	10 4
90	7 8
95	5 0
100	0

FIG. NO. 21.

DIAGRAM SHOWING POSITION OF GASBAGS AT VARYING CONDITIONS OF INFLATION.

AS 4751

About half a ton of lift was gained by the pressure stretching. The firm decided to change as many of the bags as possible, and by the 11th November the following new bags had been put into the ship: Nos. 1, 2, 3, 6, 9, 13, 14, 15, 16 and 17, giving a total weight saved of 852¾ lbs. The bags were changed one at a time, the adjoining bags being let down to about 75 per cent. full.

The lift of the ship was taken on 16th November, and results were worked out as detailed below.

On the occasion of this trial the barometer was 30·05 in., the temperature 42° F., and the mean purity of the ship 97·03 per cent. By trial under these conditions, with the ship 100 per cent. full, the disposable lift was found to be 4·45 tons.

Converting the actual disposable lift under the conditions of the trial to those in the specification, viz., barometer 29·5 in., temperature 55° F., then the disposable lift 100 per cent. full would equal—

$$\frac{884{,}443 \times 69{\cdot}1}{2{,}240} - 24 = 3{\cdot}4 \text{ tons.}$$

The purity of the hydrogen in the bags on that date was as follows:—

Number of Bag.	Purity.	Volume of Bag.	Volume of Hydrogen.
	Per Cent.	c.f.	c.f.
1	97·53	16,611	16,200
2	97·50	52,934	51,500
3	97·60	61,986	60,490
4	96·23	61,759	59,400
5	96·50	61,999	59,800
6	97·70	62,479	61,000
7	97·05	61,449	59,600
8	97·05	63,962	62,000
9	97·60	61,986	60,500
10	97·35	61,581	59,800
11	96·52	63,527	61,300
12	97·06	60,732	58,900
13	97·06	62,479	60,510
14	97·46	57,893	56,200
15	97·06	41,603	40,400
16	97·40	24,454	23,800
17	96·86	7,009	6,780
		884,443	858,180

$$\text{Mean purity} = \frac{858{,}180 \times 100}{884{,}443}$$

$$= 97{\cdot}03 \text{ per cent.}$$

A comparison of the trials of lift on 16th November and 26th November shows that when kept topped up the ship loses 40·3 lbs. lift per diem under the conditions of temperature and barometer given in the specification.

16th November 1916.—By trial, the disposable lift was found to be :—

4·45 tons,

when barometer	= 30·05 in.	*i.e.*, lift per 1,000
when temperature	= 42° F.	c.f. of hydrogen
when purity	= 97·03 per cent.	= 72·1 lbs.

Assuming the volume of the ship to be—

875,000 cubic feet

then, under the conditions of the trial,

$$\frac{875 \times 72 \cdot 1}{2{,}240} \text{ tons} = \text{total available lift}$$
$$= 28 \cdot 2 \text{ tons.}$$

Therefore, 28·2 — 4·45 tons = weight of ship

= 23·75 tons.

Now, at the specified barometer and temperature (viz., 29·5 in. and 55° F.), the lift per 1,000 cubic feet of hydrogen of 97·03 per cent. purity

= 69·1 lbs.

Therefore, under the conditions of the specification,

$$\frac{875 \times 69 \cdot 1}{2{,}240} \text{ tons} = \text{available lift}$$
$$= 27 \cdot 0 \text{ tons.}$$

Therefore, 27·0 — 23·75 tons = disposable lift under conditions of specification

= 3·25 tons.

26th November 1916.—By trial, the disposable lift was found to be—

3·74 tons,

when barometer	= 29·55 in.	*i.e.*, lift per 1,000
when temperature	= 43° F.	c.f. of hydrogen
when purity	= 96·4 per cent.	= 70·33 lbs.

But, since the last test, 0·089 ton had been taken out of the ship.

Therefore, 3·74 — 0·089 tons = true disposable lift

= 3·65 tons.

Under the conditions of the specification, the lift per 1,000 cubic feet of hydrogen of 96·4 per cent. purity

= 68·65 lbs.

Therefore, under the conditions of the specification,

$$\frac{875 \times 68 \cdot 65}{2{,}240} \text{ tons} = \text{available lift}$$
$$= 26 \cdot 82 \text{ tons.}$$

Therefore, 26·82 — 23·75 tons = disposable lift

= 3·07 tons.

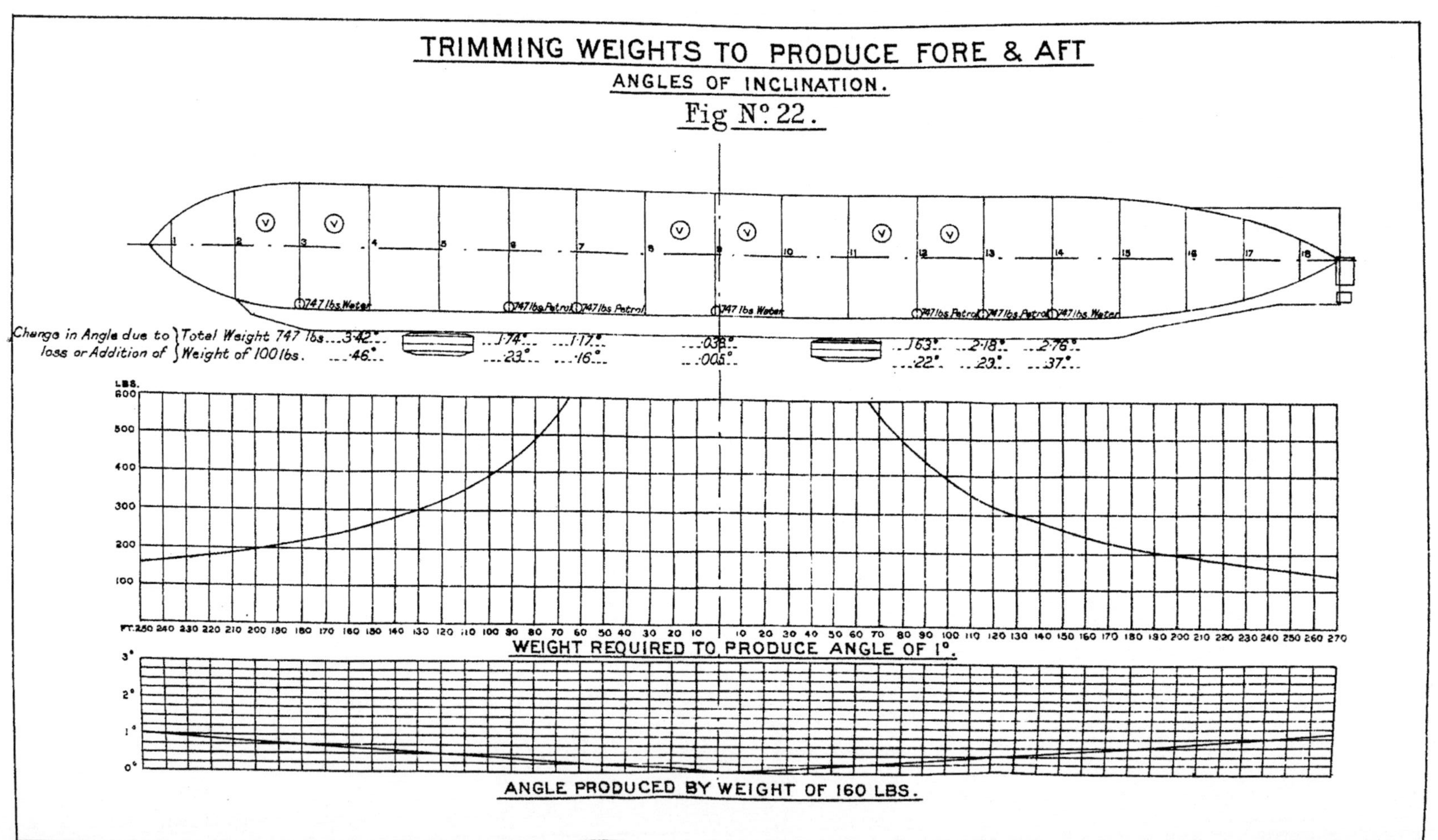
TRIMMING WEIGHTS TO PRODUCE FORE & AFT
ANGLES OF INCLINATION.
Fig No. 22.
747 lbs Water
747 lbs Petrol
747 lbs Petrol
747 lbs Water
747 lbs Petrol
747 lbs Petrol
747 lbs Water
Change in Angle due to loss or Addition of Total Weight 747 lbs. 3·42° 1·74° 1·17° ·038° 1·63° 2·18° 2·76°
Weight of 100 lbs. ·46° ·23° ·16° ·005° ·22° ·23° ·37°
LBS.
WEIGHT REQUIRED TO PRODUCE ANGLE OF 1°.
ANGLE PRODUCED BY WEIGHT OF 160 LBS.
7271.
Malby & Sons. Lith.

Therefore, under the conditions of the specification,

3·25 — 3·07 tons = loss in lift by loss in purity
= 403 lbs. in ten days.

Or the loss of lift by loss in purity of H.M.A., R. No. 9 when she is kept topped up is 40·3 lbs. per diem.

Trim Experiment.—At the time of the first experiment, after the ship had been trimmed as nearly level as possible, battens were erected at lower keel joints at frames 3 and 15—the extremes of the parallel part of the ship—and the heights above the floor of the shed measured. These were—

At 3 - - - - - - 13 ft. 11½ in.
At 15 - - - - - - 13 ft. 2½ in.

Three 56-lb. weights were then transferred from frame 9 to the forward car (*i.e.*, to frame 5), representing a moment to change trim of 3 × 56 × 4 × 30 = 20,160 lb.-ft.

The heights registered at the battens were then :—

At 3 - - - - - - 11 ft. 6 ins.
At 15 - - - - - - 13 ft. 11½ in.

Representing a total change of trim of 38½ in. in 360 ft., or approximately ½°.

Hence the moment to change trim 1° is approximately 39,500 ft.-lbs., which corresponds to shifting a man (of 160 lbs.) through approximately 250 ft.

The first trial flight and also the speed trials were carried out in the months of November and December. These are fully described in the next chapter, together with the modifications adopted for obtaining increased lift. The ship was laid up on January 5th, 1917, for these alterations, and a measurement of lift was taken the day before, giving the appended results :—

Bar., 29·86 in.; temp., 43° Fahr.; bags, 97·6 per cent. full (approx.); average purity of bags, 95·7 per cent.; damp conditions in shed.

Lift as measured, 6,132·4 lbs. = 2·73 tons.
This gives full 3·38 tons.

Lift per 1,000 c.f. under existing conditions -	70·45 lbs.
Lift per 1,000 c.f. under standard conditions -	68·15 lbs.
Difference - - - - -	2·30 lbs.

To be subtracted to bring to standard conditions, say, 2,000 lbs.

	3·38 tons.
Less - - - - - - -	·90
	2·50 tons.
At 95 per cent. full (spec. conditions) - -	1·30
Disposable lift - - - - - -	1·2 tons.

A table showing the purity of the hydrogen in the gasbags on the same day is given.

No. of Bag.	Purity. Per cent.	No. of Bag.	Purity. Per cent.
1	93·00	10	96·25
2	96·20	11	95·20
3	96·10	12	96·00
4	95·90	13	95·00
5	94·3	14	96·25
6	96·30	15	94·70
7	96·25	16	96·00
	96·50	17	88·40
9	95·70		

Mean purity of hydrogen in ship, 95·80 per cent.

Mean purity on November 8th, 1916, 97·03 per cent.

Loss in purity per diem, 0·025 per cent.

All the bags having been changed, with the exception of Nos. 14, 15, and 16, and No. 17 having been taken out and repaired, re-inflation commenced on March 7th.

An official test of the lift and trim was taken on March 17th, the results of which go to prove that ·7 ton more disposable lift was obtained than was required by the terms of the contract, and 1·7 tons above the amount of lift obtained at the trial of November 16th.

The lift was measured with all gasbags 100 per cent. full. Bar., 30·28 in.; temp., 43° Fahr.

Total lift under these conditions found to be 6·3 tons.

Reduced to equivalent at standard bar. and temp., 5·1 tons. Equivalent at 95 per cent. full = 3·8 tons.

Disposable lift at 95 per cent. full required by contract = 3·1 tons.

Comparison with previous Official Test, 16th November 1916.

Particulars.	16th November 1916.	17th March 1917.
Disposable lift 100 per cent. full, standard conditions.	3·4 tons	5·1 tons
95 per cent. full - - - - -	2·1 tons	3·8 tons
Above or below Contract 3·1 tons -	1 ton below	·7 ton above

Actual Gain in Lift by Alterations.

Particulars.	Tons.
Saving in weight by alterations to machinery - -	1·35
Saving in weight and lift by fitting spare gasbags -	·35
Total - - - - - - -	1·70 tons.

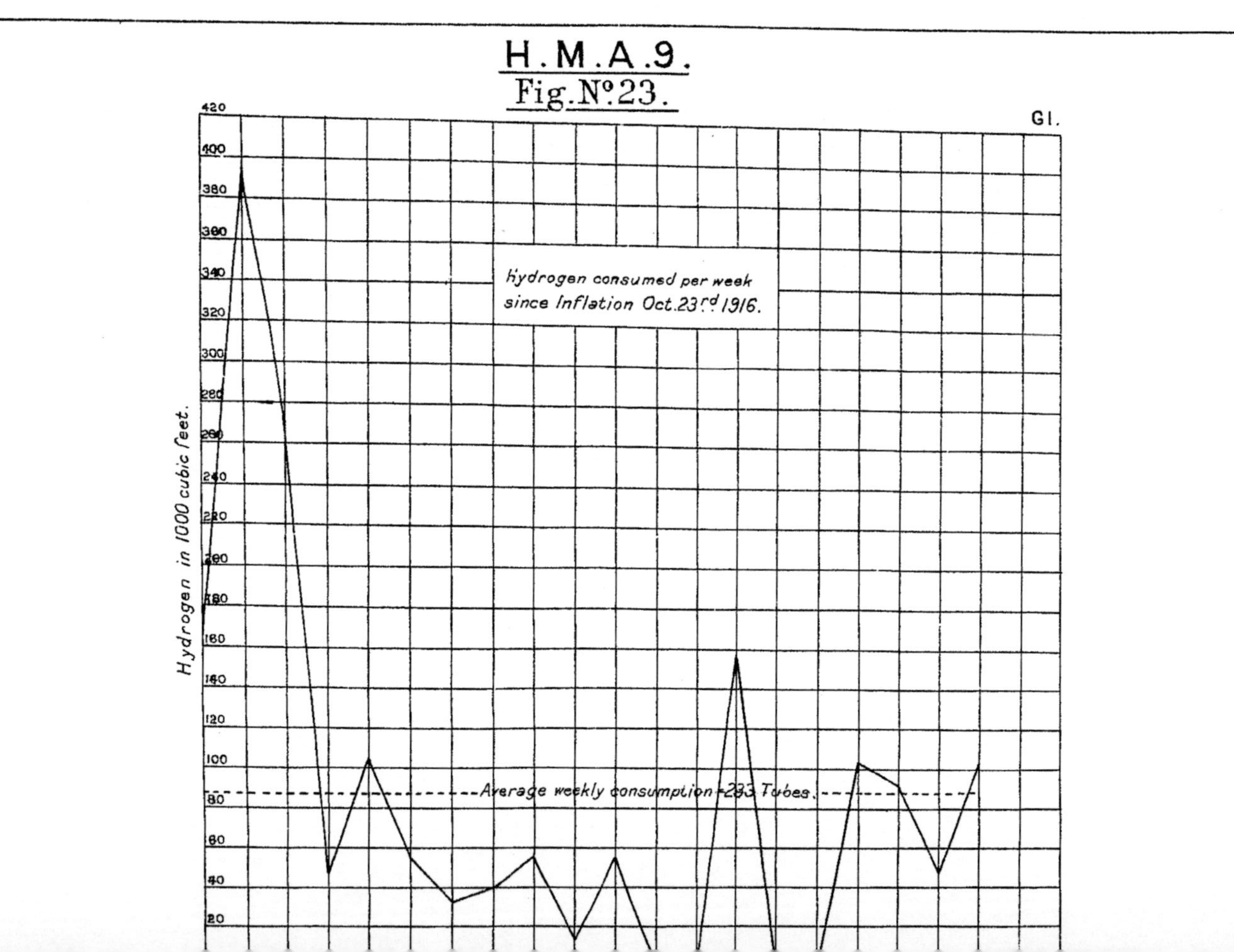
H.M.A.9.
Fig. Nº 23.
G1.
Hydrogen consumed per week since Inflation Oct. 23rd 1916.
Average weekly consumption 233 Tubes.
Hydrogen in 1000 cubic feet.
420
400
380
360
340
320
300
280
260
240
220
200
180
160
140
120
100
80
60
40
20

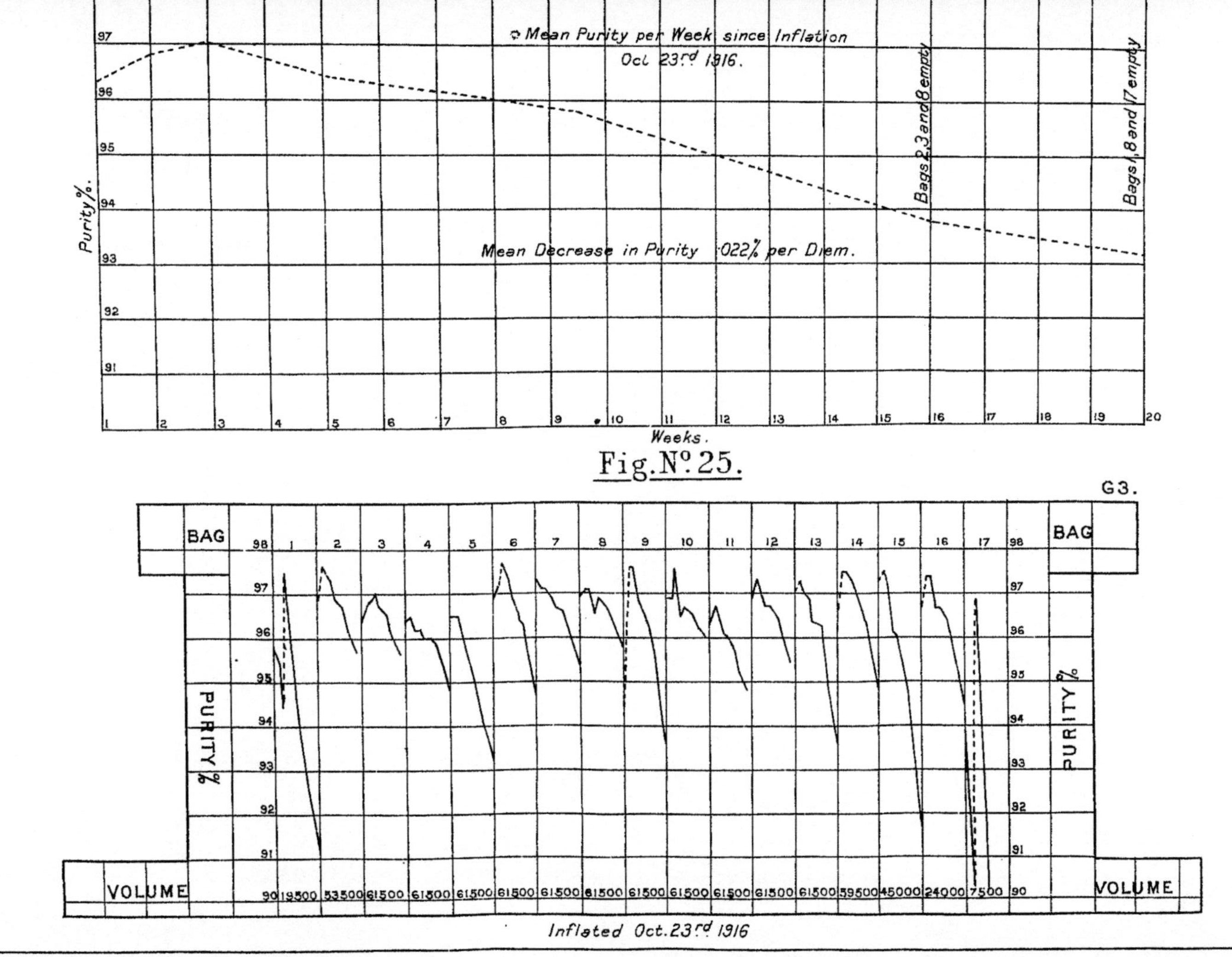

Fig. No. 25.

7271

Malby & Sons, Lith.

Graphical Analysis of the Hydrogen Consumption and Purity Decrease of H.M.A., R. No. 9.

Fig. No. 23 shows the consumption of hydrogen per week for 20 weeks from the inflation of the ship on October 23rd, 1916.

It will be observed that during the first four weeks the consumption was higher than during the later weeks. This was due to changing bags Nos. 1, 2, 6, 9, 13, 14, 15, 16, and 17. The changing of a bag not only necessitates its deflation, but, owing to the deleterious effect of gasbag-end pressure on the transverse frame, the bags on either side of the one to be deflated have to be half deflated.

Besides the deflation and changing of the above-mentioned bags, during this period more than the normal consumption of hydrogen took place owing to valve tests.

Although the original consumption of gas is in excess of what will probably be met with later, the consumption from the tenth to the fifteenth week was considerably less, as the ship was not maintained " topped up," in the case of those bags which were ultimately to be changed, during the time the alterations to the ship were in progress. Therefore the average weekly consumption, viz., 87,500 cubic feet, or 233 tubes, is not regarded as being in excess of the amount which will be required when the ship is flying.

Fig. No. 24 shows the mean purity of the ship every week for the first 20 weeks from the date of inflation.

The rise in mean purity between the first and third week was due to the changing and re-inflation of bags.

The mean decrease in purity, viz., 0·022 per cent. per diem, is considered to be less than that which will be met with when this ship is in flying commission, as the new bags, though 1,900 lbs. lighter than the original bags, are probably inferior to those in gas-retaining properties.

Fig. No. 25 shows the decrease in purity of each bag over a period of 100 days from the date of inflation.

It will be observed that the bags of small volume, viz., Nos. 1 and 17, decrease at a greater rate than the larger bags in the parallel portion of the ship. This is due to their smaller volume in comparison with the surface area, and also to the fact that the end bags have an unprotected end.

The dotted lines on this graph indicate re-inflation.

The volumes given at the foot of this graph for each bag are slightly less than the volumes of the bags now in the ship, but it is anticipated that the sum of these volumes is within 10,000 cubic feet of the present total volume.

The rise in purity of an individual bag is due to a bag on one side of it having been totally deflated, necessitating the partial deflation and subsequent re-inflation of the bag in question. This is clearly illustrated in the case of bags Nos. 8 and 10, which show a marked purity rise caused by their partial deflation and re-inflation, due to the changing of bag No. 9.

Log of Construction.

10th June 1913.—Order given to Vickers to construct. (D.W. 0243.)

18th January 1915.—Minute ordering suspension of construction. (C.P. 01513/15.)

7th February 1915.—Ensuing letter to Messrs. Vickers. (Same paper.)

June 1915.—Decision to resume building.

28th August 1915.—Official letter to Messrs. Vickers ordering resumption. (C.P. 04915/15.)

5th February 1916.—Longitudinal girders for parallel portion completed and ready for erection.

19th February 1916.—Three 90 ft. 0 in. sections, 3 to 6, 7 to 10, and 11 to 14, completed in cradles with longitudinal girders for joining up.

1st April 1916.—Bow cap fitted to structure.

8th April.—Section 1 to 2 completed. 15 to 16, 16 to 17 joined up.

22nd April 1916.—After end point completed.

6th May 1916.—Ship in two sections. Bow to 10, 11 to stern.

	1916.
Hull structure, 30 ft. frame sections (complete) joined up complete with wiring on cradles -	22nd May.
Final examination and passing of framework by overseers - - - - - - - - -	2nd June.
Rigging and adjusting nets in framework completed - - - - - - - - - -	27th June.
Hull framework lifted off cradles and slung to roof - - - - - - - - - -	28th June.
Fitting on keel in 30 ft. sections and attaching suspension wires commenced - - - -	2nd July.
First gondola arrived at Walney shed - -	5th July.
Both gondolas in place under ship - - -	8th July.
Difficulties occurring with top gas valves - -	August.
Station and grounds ready for trials - - -	15th August.
Trial of empty gasbag in place - - - -	19th August.
Gas valve seating modified satisfactorily - -	22nd August.
First run of engines in foremost gondola - -	28th August.
Fitting propeller gear boxes, transmission shafts, propeller brackets, thrust struts, petrol tanks, controls, &c. - - - - - - - - -	30th August.
Commenced lightening ship by taking things out	4th September.
First gasbag valve complete—passed - - - -	7th September.
Fitting controls and running electrical circuits -	September.
Commenced placing gasbags in ship - - -	16th September.
Six-hour machinery trial foremost gondola -	17th September.
Trouble experienced with propeller gear wheels	17/27 September.

	1916.
Ten gasbags placed in ship - - - - -	20th Sept.
One hour's machinery trial foremost gondola. All bags placed, except Nos. 1 and 17 - -	27th Sept.
Commenced inflation - - - - - -	5th October.
Commenced putting on outer cover - - -	9th October.
Inflated to 85 per cent. full - - - - -	11th October.
Inflated to 92 per cent. full - - - - -	12th October.
Commenced testing gas valves. Transverse girders at frame 3 buckled - - - - -	12th October.
Girder test using bag No. 7 - - - - -	13th October.
Lift crisis - - - - - - - - -	October.
Testing gasbag valves - - - - - -	15–19 October.
Changing gasbags for spares—	
No. 15 - - - - - - - - - -	25–26 October.
Nos. 14, 16 - - - - - - - - -	26–27 October.
Nos. 2, 13 - - - - - - - - -	27–28 October.
No. 9 - - - - - - - - - -	30th October.
No. 6 - - - - - - - - - -	3rd November.
Nos. 1, 17 - - - - - - - - -	10th–11th Nov.
Trial party joined - - - - - - -	6th November.
Carried out air-borne shed trial - - -	12th November.
Tested water ballast controls - - -	15th November.
Ship completed - - - - - - -	19th November.
Ship ready for flight - - - - - - -	21st November.
First trial flight - - - - - - -	27th November.
Ship provisionally accepted by Admiralty - -	12th December.
Speed trial flight - - - - - - -	13th December.
	1917.
Ship laid up for alteration - - - -	5th January.
Trial party left - - - - - - -	10th January.
Ship slung to roof of shed - - - - -	18th January.
Changing gasbags for spares—	
No. 11 - - - - - - - - - -	19th January.
Nos. 10, 12 - - - - - - - - -	20th January.
No. 7 - - - - - - - - - -	21st January. 6th February.
No. 8 (for linen bag) - - - - - -	7th–8th Feb.
Nos. 1, 2, 3, 4, and 5 - - - - -	During Feb.
All bags changed and in, except bag for No. 5 -	By 1st March.
Alterations to after gondola machinery, &c. -	Jan., Feb., March.
Commenced re-inflation - - - - - -	7th March.
Trial of machinery in shed - - - - -	13th March.
Valves (gasbag) tested and correct - - -	15th March.
Ship completed - - - - - - - -	17th March.
Trial flight after alterations - - - - -	23rd March.
Ship ready to leave Barrow - - - - -	27th March.
Ship left for Howden - - - - - -	4th April.

CHAPTER VIII.

First Flights and Alterations after Trials.

On 16th November 1916 the airship was practically ready for flight. On that day the official test of the lift and trim of the ship was taken, and, as has been explained in the previous chapter, these experiments proved that the ship was short of practically one ton of disposable lift as defined in the terms of the contract. It was considered that weight could be cut down by adopting the following measures :—

1. Removing one engine from the after gondola and using the remaining engine to drive direct a propeller at the after end of the car.
2. Fitting single plane rudders and elevators.
3. Changing the remaining old bags for new spare bags.
4. Substituting duralumin tubes for the steel tubes in the keel if the ship would stand it.

The question then arose as to whether these alterations should be immediately put in hand, or a trial flight undertaken with the ship in her existing condition, for the purpose of gaining experience of her behaviour in the air.

The latter course was adopted and, on 21st November, the ship was completed and ready for her trial flight. The next day appeared suitable for the trial, but the wind was slightly too strong, varying between 12 and 17 miles per hour. There were also considerable variations in temperature.

First Trial Flight.

A suitable opportunity occurred on 27th November. Early in the morning the barometer was 30·1 in., temperature about 39° F., wind N.W. by N., about 10 m.p.h., the sky clear and visibility good.

Preparations to take the ship out were commenced at 8 a.m. The ship was balanced up in the shed with 16 men on board, fuel for three hours at full power arranged so that the forward engines had fuel for four hours and the after engines for two hours (to assist the trim, the ship being inclined to be " tail heavy "), and a sufficient quantity of water ballast disposed in three spare petrol tanks, one forward, one amidships, and one aft.

The gasbags were about 97 per cent. full.

The ship was taken out of the shed and walked over to No. 4 mooring bollard, the only incident worth recording being that the forward buffer wheels under the foremost gondola broke off when crossing the rail of the shed door. This was due to a duralumin forging carrying away in both cases.

On reaching No. 4 bollard the ship was balanced up again, the sun having a warming effect on the gas, and it was necessary to put extra ballast in the after car before leaving the ground.

To face p. 50.

PLATE NO. 41.

H.M.A. R. NO. 9 LEAVING SHED FOR INITIAL TRIAL FLIGHT, NOVEMBER 27TH, 1916.

The ship left the ground just light, assisted by a discharge of about 80 lbs. of water ballast forward.

The after propellers were started almost immediately, and the ship rose gradually to about 200 ft. The forward propellers were started soon after leaving the ground, and the ship headed out to sea, the height being gradually increased to 500 ft.

Shortly after getting over the sea it was noticed that the ship was not answering her helm properly, and it was observed that the auxiliary rudders were flapping about and not under control. It appears that the pedestal carrying the auxiliary control wheel in the after gondola had buckled, the control wires had stretched, become loose, and had come off their sheaves. The rudders, consequently, were free to flap about.

At first, the starboard and port units flapped together, the opposite way to the way the main steering rudders were put over. Eventually the two units took up opposite positions, each pointing inboard, that is to say the port unit had starboard helm on and the starboard unit port helm. Orders were given to secure the auxiliary rudders amidships. This was done in about half an hour after carrying away.

The ship was by this time over Morecambe Bay, at a height of about 900 ft., and was getting lighter.

Mr. Pratt, representing Messrs. Vickers, went right aft to the reducing boxes of the rudder and elevator controls and found that both were working correctly. He then went up the climbing tube to the gun platform and found it was comfortable to stand there. He stated that there would be no difficulty in working a Lewis gun from that position. The ship turned in Morecambe Bay and headed back towards the landing ground.

As down helm was required on the elevators, it was evident that the ship was getting light, and bags Nos. 2, 3, 8, and 9 were each valved for 8 seconds.

As the ship approached the landing ground height was gradually reduced, but, on slowing up speed, the ship commenced to rise, and arrived over No. 4 bollard practically stationary at a height of 300 ft., rising. The trail rope was not dropped and the propellers were put ahead again for another circuit. Bags 2, 3, 8, and 9 were valved as before. At the second attempt the ship reached the landing party and the trail rope was dropped from a height of 150 ft.

The ship did not quite reach the landing party, and commenced to rise. The forward propellers were then swivelled down and the ship prevented from rising until the landing party reached the trail rope. This was "snatched" at No. 3 bollard, and the ship was hauled down by the landing party, gas being valved to assist them. The ship was thereupon walked into the shed without further incident.

The rough log, measurements of lift before and after flight, consumption of oil and petrol used during flight, and list of crew and their stations are now set forth in detail.

Rough Log.

Trial Flight, 27th November 1916.

9.20 a.m.—Ballasted up in shed.
9.31 ,, .—Left shed.
9.36 ,, .—Clear of doors.
9.46 ,, .—At mooring block No. 4, ballasted up again.
10.00 ,, .—Started up engines.
10.4 ,, .—Left ground. In clutch. Proceeded. 1,000 revs., both cars.
10.10 ,, .—Auxiliary rudder controls broke loose.
10.25 ,, .—Off coastguard station south end of Walney Island. Course—East. 700 ft. Maximum height over Morecambe Bay, 900 ft. Pressure in bags ½ mm.
11.5 ,, .—Stopped engines over No. 4 mooring block. Ship light. Missed landing party. Proceeded for new landing. 600 ft. Turned, helm hard-a-port. Took 3 mins. to turn 180 degs. (Judged diameter of turning circle about 1½ miles.)
11.19 ,, .—Dropped foremost trail rope. Still light. Swivelled down with forward propellers.
11.27 ,, .—Landed at No. 3 bollard.
11.40 ,, .—Inside windscreen.
11.44 ,, .—Entered shed.

Measurements of Lift before and after Flight, November 1916.

Before.—November 26th, 1916.

Conditions: Ship full of gas. Barometer, 29.55 ins. Temperature dry, 43° F., wet 41° F.

	Lbs.
Water ballast (three tanks all full) - -	3,870
Forward car :—	
Ballast - - - - - - - -	1,520
Fuel, &c. - - - - - - - -	1,060
Planks in walking-way - - - -	336
After car :	
Ballast - - - - - - - -	542
Fuel, &c. - - - - - - - -	1,052
Total - - - - -	8,380 lbs.

N.B.—The dynamo and the fabric water ballast bags had been taken out since the official test made November 16th, 1916.

After.—November 27th, 1916.

Conditions : Bags about 97 per cent. full. Barometer 30.21 in. Temperature 40° F.

	Lbs.
Water ballast in tanks - - - - -	2,910
Ballast (iron and sand) :	
Forward - - - - - - - -	1,806
Aft - - - - - - - - -	1,360
Fuel and oil - - - - - - -	1,314
Total - - - - -	7,390 lbs.

N.B.—Water in radiators (660 lbs.) is taken as being included in the fixed weights.

Consumption of Petrol and Oil during Trial Flight—November 1916.

	Galls.
Forward car :	
Petrol used - - - - - - - -	33.00
Oil used :—	
P. engine - - - - - - - -	1·25
S. engine - - - - - - - -	1·25
P. lower gear box - - - - - -	·75
S. lower gear box - - - - - -	·125
P. propeller gear box - - - - -	·75
S. propeller gear box - - - - -	·35
After car :	
Petrol used - - - - - - - -	27.00
Oil used :—	
P. engine - - - - - - - -	·50
S. engine - - - - - - - -	1·00
P. lower gear box - - - - - -	·30
S. lower gear box - - - - - -	·30
P. propeller gear box - - - - -	·125
S. propeller gear box - - - - -	·25

List and Stations of Crew—27th November 1916.

Forward car :

Wing Captain E. A. Masterman -	Pilot.
Mr. B. S. Brice, W.O. II. - -	Elevator control.
C.P.O. Cook - - - - -	Helmsman.
P.O. Robinson - - - - -	Ballast, telegraphs, controls.
Mr. J. Watson (of Messrs. Vickers) C.P.O. Mathewson - - - A.M. 1 Turley - - - -	Engines.
Eng. Lieut. Commdr. G. Villar -	Machinery generally.
C.P.O. Miller - - - - -	Above foremost car in keel.
C.P.O. Coward - - - - -	W/T cabin.
Mr. H. Pratt (representing Messrs. Vickers) - - - - - -	Near W/T cabin.

After car :

Squadron Commdr. T. K. Elmsley	Assistant Pilot.
C.P.O. Mathews - - - - -	Helm (secondary control).
L. M. Smith - - - - -	Telephones, &c.
Mr. A. Bushfield, W.O. II. - -	Engines.
C.P.O. Simmons - - - - -	Engines.

The following are the principal features noticed on the flight :—

Speed.—No observations of speed were made. The engines were not run at more than 1,000 revolutions per minute, but the general impression was that the ship was rather slow. It is assumed to have been about 35 m.p.h.

Navigability.—The elevators controlled the ship for height satisfactorily. 0° to 5° helm on the elevators was found to give a total range of inclination of 10° on the ship.

The ship reached maximum angles of 10° down and 5° up in flight.

The rudders were not so satisfactory. The ship was sluggish in answering her helm, and, on one occasion, took three minutes to turn 180°. At 35 m.p.h. this gives a turning circle of 1·1 miles diameter.

Outer Cover.—With regard to this, observations made from the ground reveal the following facts :—

Half-way between 2 and 3 frames under pressure.

Abaft 3 to 3½ region of low pressure, fabric bulged outwards.

Abaft that to 15 all more or less under pressure.

Aft of 15 region of low pressure. On the bottom half of the hull in this region the keel and outer covers flapped rather badly in wake of the after propellers.

Swivelling Propellers.—The value of these, especially those fitted forward, was apparent.

Engines.—These ran satisfactorily and well throughout the flight. One sparking plug in the starboard after engine became defective after one hour's flight. The engines were run at speeds varying from 800 to 1,000 r.p.m.

As a result of the trial several modifications and alterations were considered necessary. Among minor details the following are considered to be worthy of mention :—

1. Change Nos. 10, 11, and 12 gasbags for spares.
2. Replace top gas valves by Zeppelin type side valves in bags Nos. 1, 2, and 3, to allow of gunfire.
3. Securing of outer cover aft.
4. Change climbing tube for stiffer tube.
5. New propeller gear boxes.
6. Fit improved multiplying gear for elevator and rudder controls.
7. New propellers of increased pitch required forward.

Acceptance of Ship.

The question of the acceptance of the ship now arose. Messrs. Vickers stated they would not be in a position to lay her up for the alteration to the machinery in the after gondola for a period of six weeks. It was considered desirable that the ship should be used during this period, provided the lift was maintained and weather conditions were favourable. It was finally decided that the ship should be taken over by the Admiralty from 2 p.m. December 12th, on the understanding that Messrs. Vickers carried out the following obligations, which, for the sake of brevity, have been condensed :—

1. That the contract obligations, as laid down in the original contract, and modifications agreed to between the firm and the Admiralty were carried out.

2. That the guaranteed lift should be obtained by substituting the 240-h.p. Maybach engine recovered from L 33 for the two original engines, with one propeller directly driven aft of the car.

3. That the necessary speed should be obtained.

4. All alterations agreed to, prior to the date of taking over, to be carried out.

Speed Trials.

Two speed trials were undertaken the following day—December 13th. For this purpose two stations were selected at the North and South ends of Walney Island, at a distance of 6·802 miles apart. The magnetic bearing of the two points was ascertained to be approximately N. 4° 10′ W. Observing parties were placed at these two stations, equipped with a "Verey" light signalling apparatus, by means of which a signal could be made to the ship at the instant she crossed the sighting line of the station.

The first flight was made in the morning. The crew consisted partly of the trial staff and partly of No. 9's proper crew. In addition, Mr. Evans, representing the D.N.C., and Mr. Wallis, representing Messrs. Vickers, Ltd., were taken up. In all 16 persons were carried. The ship was balanced up in the shed. Two hours' supply of petrol was carried both in the forward and after tanks, and 2,170 lbs. of water ballast.

At 10.45 the ship left the ground and quickly rose to an altitude of 600 feet, and headed in a northerly direction to get up to the northernmost station. The first trial run from north to south was begun, but shortly after passing the northernmost station the same trouble was experienced with the auxiliary rudders as on the occasion of the first trial flight. The trial run was abandoned, and the auxiliary rudders having been secured as well as possible, the ship was headed for the landing ground, landed and taken into the shed.

A brief conference was held and it was decided to completely remove the auxiliary rudder system. Messrs. Vickers' workmen carried this out during the dinner hour. The gas lost on the previous trip was made up, fuel supply and water ballast replenished, and, with the same crew as on the previous trip, the ship was taken out of the shed.

At 2.30 p.m. she left the ground, and, rising to a height of 600 feet, she headed for the northernmost station. The steering was found to be much improved by the removal of the auxiliary rudders.

Two runs were made, from north to south, and south to north respectively. Everything passed off successfully, with the exception that at the finish of the second run an oil pipe for the gear boxes of the after engine burst, necessitating the ship landing with three engines.

The forward propellers appeared to absorb the full power of the engines fairly satisfactorily at 1,250 revolutions, but the after propellers, being in the current of air from the forward ones, could have been run up to 1,400 revolutions.

The following is a tabulated statement of the two trial runs :—

First Run.

Left shed - - - -	10.20 a.m.
Left ground - - -	10.45 a.m.
Landed - - - -	11.45 a.m.

Second Run.

Left shed - - - -	2.12 p.m.
Left ground - - -	2.31 p.m.
Passed N. station - -	2.45 p.m.

First Trial Run, from N. end to S. end.

Time - - - - -	7 mins. 57·8 secs.
R.P.M.—forward car - -	1,250.
after car - -	1,250.
Speed - - - -	About 52 m.p.h.
Wind - - - -	About 6–8 m.p.h. N.W.

Second Trial Run, from S. end to N. end.

Time - - - - -	12 mins. 35·2 secs.
Passed south station - -	At 3·5 p.m.
R.P.M.—forward car - -	1,250.
after car - -	1,300.
Wind about 9 m.p.h., direction about N.W.	
Speed - - - -	About 31 m.p.h.
Landed - - - -	3.40 p.m.
In shed - - - -	3.55 p.m.

Course.

Length - - - -	6·802 miles.
Bearing - - - -	About N. 4° 10′ W. (Mag.).

The Admiralty formula for determining the speed of the ship is as follows :—

$$\text{Mean speed} = \sqrt{V_1 \times V_2 + W^2}.$$

When V_1 = speed in one direction.
V_2 = speed in opposite direction.
W = velocity of wind.

To face p. 56.

PLATE NO. 42.

H.M.A. R. NO. 9 ON LANDING GROUND.

Taking the velocity of the wind for both runs at ·9 miles per hour the formula gives the following results :—

$$\text{Mean speed of ship} = \sqrt{51 \cdot 4 \times 32 \cdot 5 + 9^2}.$$
$$= 41 \cdot 8 \; m.p.h.$$

Owing to irregularities in course, due to wind variation, it is probable that the actual mean speed of the ship slightly exceeded this figure, and may be taken as being in the neighbourhood of 42·5 m.p.h.

Alterations to Ship.

After the second of these trial flights a meeting was held, and the representatives of Messrs. Vickers considered that the speed of the ship would not be adversely affected by substituting the single Maybach engine as had been previously suggested for increasing the disposable lift.

Admiralty approval was obtained for carrying out this alteration on December 26th, and on January 5th, 1917, the ship was laid up for the work to be commenced. From this date to March 17th, the work was in progress and the alterations to machinery and after gondola were carried out in the manner described in a previous chapter. Various other alterations were also put in hand during this period, of which the following were the most important :—

Steel oil delivery pipes were fitted in place of the copper ones, with an " S " bend to prevent vibration.

Multiplying gear was fitted to the rudder and elevator controls.

Repairs to the buffer landing wheels on the forward gondola. Steel crossheads were used to replace the defective duralumin forgings.

A new and stiffer form of climbing tube for access to the gun platform was fitted between the gasbags.

The keel walking way was completely repaired.

Three automatic gas valves of the Zeppelin type were fitted to bags Nos. 1, 2, and 3.

A new covering for the walking-way on the top of the ship was fitted, made of a canvas form with fabric edges stuck on to the outer cover.

The after part of the after gondola was cut out to receive the new machinery, the superstructure was altered, and new engine bearers fitted.

On January 18th the ship was slung to the roof of the shed. The following gasbags were changed : Nos. 1, 2, 3, 4, 5, 7, 8, 10, 11, and 12, and, on the 17th March, re-inflation was commenced.

The Admiralty required the following trials to be carried out as soon as the alterations were completed :—

1. Preliminary trial in the shed of about one hour's duration, at powers varying up to full power, to test gear generally.

2. Full power trial in shed of four hours' duration.

3. Flight trial of not less than one hour's duration, during which the engines were to develop full power.

Trials 1 and 3 to be carried out with the machinery of both gondolas, trial 2 with the machinery of aft gondola only.

On March 13th the one hour's full power trial with engines of the fore and aft cars was carried out. During this trial a cock and a pipe in the German oil system of the Maybach engine (aft) gave out, and these had to be replaced before the four hours' endurance trial.

This trial with the engine of the after car was started at 7 p.m. the same day, but was stopped at 7.30 owing to sparks from the silencer blowing dangerously near to a kite balloon inflated wth hydrogen on the floor of the shed. This kite balloon was deflated, and, after a lapse of time to allow the hydrogen to escape, the engine was restarted at 8.20 and ran until 9.15, when a stop had to be made to replace a broken gauge glass. A restart was made at 10.40 and the engine ran continuously for three hours, the total time run being 4¾ hours. This was accepted as equivalent to the four hours' endurance test demanded.

The German engine ran extremely well throughout the trial. Slightly more vibration was noticed than was normal; this was probably owing to the propeller shaft, which had been taken from the wrecked Zeppelin, being slightly out of truth. This was taken out and a replace shaft from Messrs. Wolseleys fitted.

The following modifications were also carried out:—

Stiffening to aft top casing of after car.
Duralumin suspension tubes replaced by steel.
Aft gear box bearers stiffened with gussets.
Car ventilation scoops refitted.

Trial Flight after Alterations.

The alterations to the ship were finally completed by Messrs. Vickers on March 17th, and a test was made to ascertain the lift and trim of the ship.

The lift was measured with all gasbags 100 per cent. full. Barometer 30·28 in. Temperature 43° F. Total lift, 6·3 tons. Reduced to equivalent at standard barometer and temperature, with gasbags 95 per cent. full, 3·8 tons.

Before alterations the lift was approximately 2·1 tons. A gain of 1·7 tons disposible lift was therefore obtained, and·6 ton in excess of the contract.

As regards trim, the ship was now up by the stern, instead of inclined up by the bow, and it was necessary to put in over 1,000 lbs. of water on frames 12 and 13 to correct this. It was decided to fit a spare petrol tank on frame 15 to obviate carrying this water ballast.

A favourable opportunity was now awaited for the one hour's flight trial. This took place on the 23rd March. The weather was fine, and the wind 12 m.p.h., almost due west.

Two speed trials were made, one in each direction, over a two miles course, and the speed attained was 43 m.p.h. During the first run the forward engines were doing 1,200 revs. per minute, and the after one 1,200. During the second run the forward engines were at 1,200 revs., while the after one was at 1,240.

After the trials the ship continued flight until the forward gear box lubrication broke down, when she was headed for the landing ground, landed, and taken into the shed.

The whole flight was most satisfactory, and a thorough examination of the keel, lower girders, cars, &c., failed to show any structural defects.

It is particularly noteworthy that the speed attained on these trials was no less than on the original trials, in spite of the fact that one engine had been removed. This was highly satisfactory, as it proved that the opinion that the speed of the ship would not be adversely affected by these alterations was completely justified.

On this occasion Squadron Commander Hicks piloted the ship, and the total number of crew and passengers was 21 men.

New lubrication arrangements were fitted to the lower gear boxes of the forward car by station ratings, as Messrs. Vickers' workmen were on strike. Oil pumps were taken from the spare Maybach engines and fittings made for attaching them to the gear boxes and for driving them by means of the old dynamo drives. These arrangements proved to be satisfactory.

Departure for Howden.

H.M.A. R. No. 9 was on March 27th entirely completed, with the exception of three outstanding items:—

1. Gas pressure gauges to be fitted.
2. New oil pumps to be fitted to forward gear boxes.
3. Spare petrol tank to be fitted to frame 15.

It had been definitely approved some time previous to this date that the ship should be stationed at Howden. It was now merely a question of waiting for suitable weather. The conditions at this period were most unsettled, low barometer being accompanied by snow.

On April 4th, however, the weather reports appeared favourable and the ship left for Howden with Squadron Commander Hicks and her proper crew on board at 11.20 a.m. She passed over Carnforth at 12.5 p.m. and at 1.30 p.m. reached Leeds. Shortly afterwards she ran into a heavy snow squall and dived at an angle of 15° which threatened to become worse. The engines were stopped and the ship righted and proceeded. 1,000 lbs. of water ballast were dropped and the ship climbed to 2,000 feet. The wind during this squall was estimated between 30 and 35 m.p.h. At 1.57 Barlow Airship Station was sighted and at 2.20 Howden was reached. The ship was ballasted up and a successful landing was made at 2.45.

All the engines were run at 1,175 revs. throughout the trip.

The ship left the ground approximately 1,000 lbs. light, with bags 98 per cent. full.

The total amount of ballast expended was 2,000 lbs.

Consumption of petrol, 994 lbs. Consumption of oil, 85·5 lbs.

Gas was valved for landing from bags Nos. 2, 3, 8, 9, 11, and 12.

In conclusion, from that date onwards up to the time of writing the ship has been stationed at Howden, where she has proved to be not only invaluable for the training of officers and men, but also in assisting to carry out the patrol of the portion of the East Coast allocated to the station.

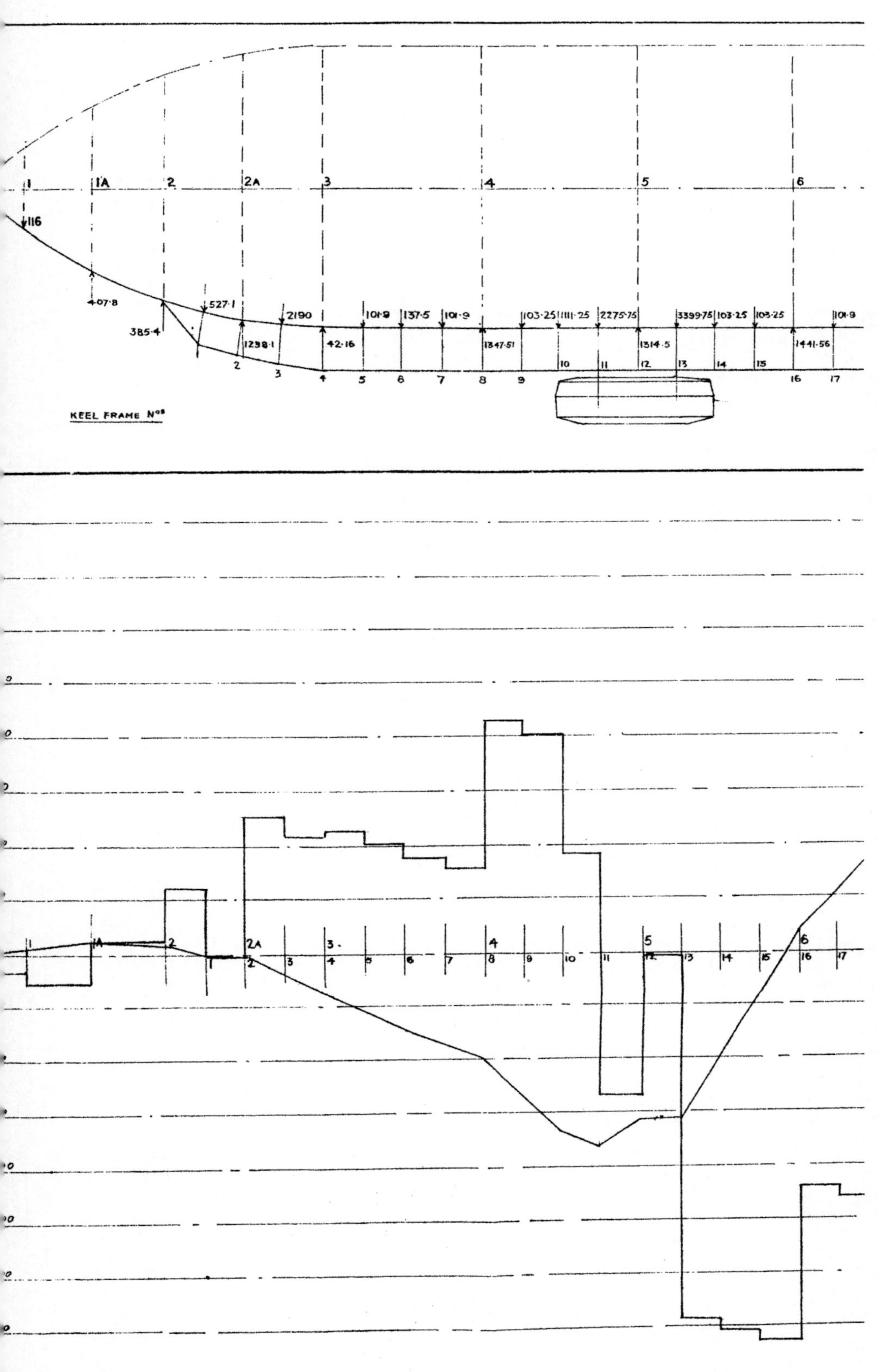

7869. Pk 2895. 250. 5. 18.

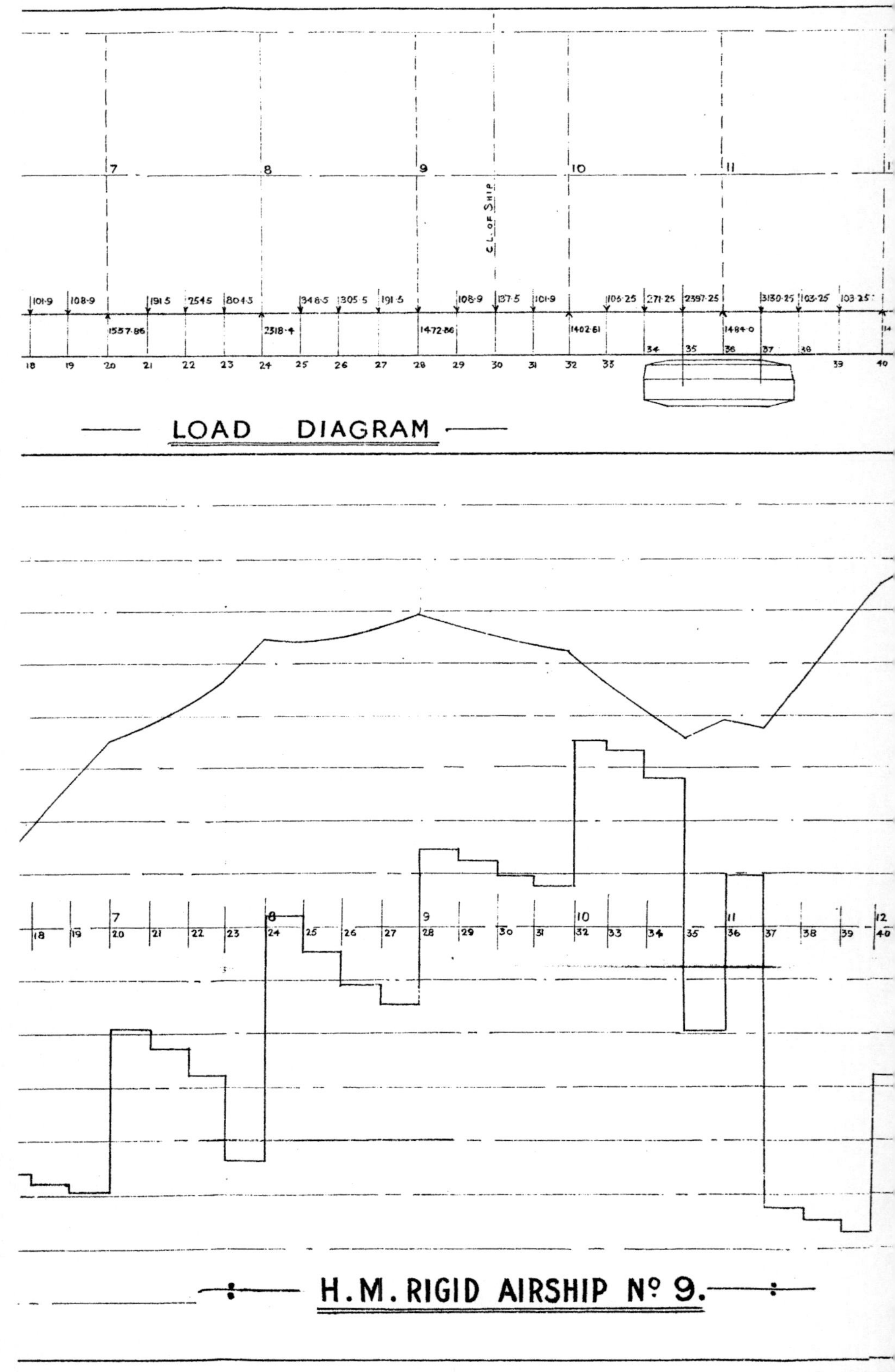

LOAD DIAGRAM
C.L. OF SHIP
101·9
108·9
191·5
254·5
804·5
348·5
305·5
191·5
108·9
137·5
101·9
106·25
271·25
2397·25
3130·25
103·25
1557·86
2318·4
1472·86
1402·61
1484·0
H.M. RIGID AIRSHIP Nº 9.

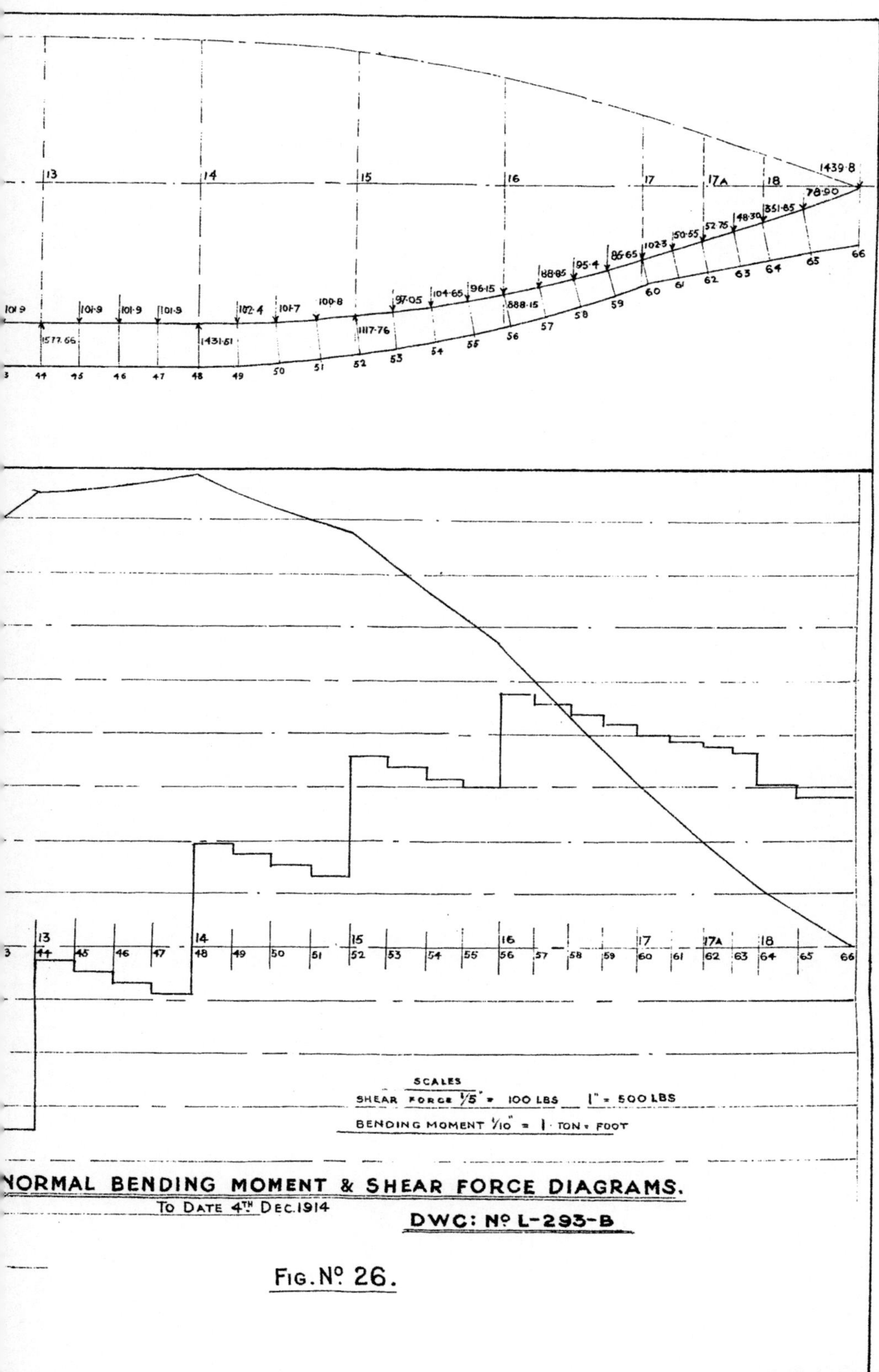
SCALES
SHEAR FORCE 1/5" = 100 LBS 1" = 500 LBS
BENDING MOMENT 1/10" = 1 TON = FOOT
NORMAL BENDING MOMENT & SHEAR FORCE DIAGRAMS.
TO DATE 4TH DEC. 1914
DWG: No L-293-B

Fig. No 26.

APPENDIX I.

ACTUAL WEIGHTS—FIXED ONLY.

	Lbs.
Duralumin framework	9,171
Wiring	1,670
Platform tubes	223
Pins	700
Rudders and elevators	1,373
Keel girder	6,792
Walking-way	320
Petrol tank girders	207
Gasbags	9,274
Nets	986
Outer cover	2,960
Miscellaneous fabric on hull	199
Car structure	2,872
Cabin	557
Fittings in cars	120
Control gear and telegraphs	666
Lighting and telephones	393
Gas valves	446
Machinery and transmission	9,800
Petrol tanks and supply tanks	967
Car suspensions and buffer wheels	396
Total	50,092

Tons.	cwts.	qrs.	lbs.
22	7	1	0

WEIGHTS OF MACHINERY, &c.

The following tables of weights of machinery &c., represent the weights with the original engines in the after gondola. The summary at the end gives the weights removed or replaced in the after car, showing the total saving effected by the alterations.

TOTAL WEIGHTS.

	Forward.	After.	Total.
Motors up to crank shaft coupling	2,058·434	2,064·028	4,122·462
Clutches and fly wheels	268·500	268·500	537·000
Shafting, gearing, &c.	1,486·460	1,600·500	3,086·960
Water in radiators, jackets and pipes	340·000	340·000	680·000
Oil in lubrication system	472·800	472·800	945·600
Fuel in service tanks	150·825	150·825	301·750
Fuel, oil, water pipes and valves, radiators and service tank.	660·2225	660·1625	1,320·385
Exhaust pipes and silencers	128·1875	128·1875	256·375
Main petrol tanks and pipes to cars	155·6000	155·6000	311·200
Telegraphs	125·2800	105·344	230·624
Fuel in storage tanks	1,826·412	1,826·412	3,652·824
Ventilation fittings and auxiliary water tanks.	12·18	12·18	24·36
Water in auxiliary tanks	76·50	76·50	153·00
Tools carried	22·00	22·00	44·00
Propellers	225·375	268·75	494·125
Totals	8,008·776	8,151·789	16,160·665

MOTORS UP TO THE COUPLINGS ON CRANK SHAFTS AND ALL FITTINGS ON MOTORS.

	No.	Forward Car.		After Car.		Total.
		Port.	Starboard.	Port.	Starboard.	
Motors up to crankshaft couplings.	4	990·657	995·97	989·5	1,002·72	3,978·847
Holding-down bolts	4 sets	1·75	1·75	1·75	1·75	7·0
Starting pumps	4	14·125	14·125	14·125	14·125	56·5
Carburettor save-alls	8	1·375	1·375	1·375	1·375	5·5
Pipe system for starting pumps.	4 sets	2·5	2·5	2·5	2·5	10·0
Starting magnetos	4	5·875	5·875	5·875	5·875	23·5
Revolution indicators with flexible shafting.	4	4·438	4·438	4·438	4·438	17·742
Starting pump conduit (discharge overboard).	4	3·312	3·312	3·312	3·312	13·248
Petrol pump save-alls		·875	·875	·875	·875	3·5
Induction pipe strainers.	4	1·656	1·656	1·656	1·656	6·625
					Total -	4,122·462

CLUTCHES.

—	No.	Forward Car.		After Car.		Total.
		Port.	Starboard.	Port.	Starboard.	
Clutch and flywheel.	4	124·000	124·000	124·000	124·000	496·000
Controls for clutch.	4	10·25	10·25	10·25	10·25	41·000
					Total -	537·000

SHAFTING-GEARING, &c.

	No.	Forward Car Port.	Forward Car Starboard.	After Car. Port.	After Car. Starboard.	Total.
Outer gear box -	4	149·375	149·25	149·00	150·00	597·625
Lower gear box -	4	109·000	108·50	163·00	163·00	543·500
Swivelling tubes -	4	275·000	279·50	279·00	282·00	1,115·500
Carden shaft -	4	51·500	51·00	51·00	51·00	204·500
Intermediate gear boxes.	2	250·000		249·500		499·500
Swivelling control -	—	53·312		52·937		106·249
Locking device for swivelling control.	2	1·1375		1·1375		2·275
Strengthening plate and bolts for outer gear boxes.	4	2·594	2·594	2·594	2·594	10·376
					Total -	3,079·525

PROPELLERS.

Propeller Number.	Where Fitted.	Weight.
B. 17749	Starboard forward -	106 lbs. 10 ozs.
B. 17746	Port forward - -	118 lbs. 12 ozs.
B. 18523	Starboard aft - -	136 lbs. 12 ozs.
B. 18522	Port aft - - -	132 lbs. 0 ozs.
	Total - - -	494·125 lbs.

WEIGHT OF WATER IN CIRCULATING PIPES, JACKETS, AND RADIATORS.

	Forward Car. Port.	Forward Car. Starboard.	After Car. Port.	After Car. Starboard.	Total.
Water in radiators and circulating pipes.	104	101	107·5	103·5	416
Water in jackets	135		129		264
				Total -	680

WEIGHT OF OIL IN LUBRICATION SYSTEM AT WORKING LEVEL.

	No.	Forward Car.		After Car.		Total.
		Port.	Starboard.	Port.	Starboard.	
Outer gear box tanks -	4	24·0	24·0	24·0	24·0	96·0
Lower gear box tanks -	4	21·2	21·2	21·2	21·2	84·8
Engine service tanks -	4	95·6	95·6	95·6	95·6	382·4
Engine reserve tanks -	4	95·6	95·6	95·6	95·6	382·4
					Total -	945·6

WEIGHT OF FUEL IN STORAGE AND SERVICE TANKS.

	No.	Forward Car.	After Car.	Total
Service tanks - - -	2	150·825	150·825	301·75
Storage tanks - - -	4	1,826·412	1,826·412	3,652·824
			Total -	3,954·574

WEIGHT OF FUEL, OIL, WATER PIPES AND VALVES WITH SERVICE TANKS, OIL COOLERS AND RADIATORS.

	No.	Forward Car.		After Car.		Total.
		Port.	Starboard.	Port.	Starboard.	
Radiators - -	4	208·000	224·000	207·500	224·500	864·000
Oil coolers with brackets.	4	4·250	4·250	4·250	4·250	17·000
Albany oil cooler pumps.	4	10·280	10·280	10·280	10·280	41·120
Service oil tanks, covers and fittings.	4	15·000	15·000	15·000	15·000	60·000
Gearbox tanks, covers and fittings.	—	6·875	6·875	6·875	6·875	27·500
Reserve box tanks, covers and fittings.	—	12·625	12·625	12·625	12·625	50·500
Fuel system, pipes and valves.	—	4·850	4·850	4·850	4·850	19·400
Oil system, pipes and valves.	—	18·970	18·840	18·970	18·840	75·620
Circulating pipes and valves.	—	27·59		27·53		55·120
Radiator screens -	—	2·4375	2·4375	2·4375	2·4375	9·750
Gear box oil coolers -	—	4·25	4·25	4·25	4·25	17·000
Oil system, pipes and valves for gear box lubrication.	—	24·1875		24·1875		48·375
Service petrol tanks -	—	17·5000		17·5000		35·000
					Total -	1320·385

WEIGHT OF EXHAUST PIPES AND SILENCERS.

	No.	Forward Car.		After Car.		Total.
		Port.	Starboard.	Port.	Starboard.	
Zeppelin type silencers.	4	61·00	61·00	61·00	61·00	244·00
Brackets and fittings.	4	3·09	3·09	3·09	3·09	12·375
					Total -	256·375

WEIGHT OF FUEL STORAGE TANKS AND PIPES TO CARS.

	No.	Forward Car.	After Car.	Total.
Fuel storage tanks - -	4	100·00	100·00	200·0
Pipes to service tanks -	4	39·85	39·85	79·5
Petrol discharge valves -	4	10·75	10·75	21·5
Vent pipes from storage tanks.	4	5·00	5·00	10·0
			Total -	311·0

TELEGRAPHS.

Instruments, chains, pulleys, &c.	109·08	91·219	200·299
Brackets, clips, &c. - - -	16·20	14·125	30·325
		Total -	230·624

WEIGHTS NOT INCLUDED IN OTHER LISTS.

	No.	Forward Car.		After Car.		Total.
		Port	Starboard.	Port.	Starboard.	
Ventilation fittings, car sub-structure.	4	20·9	2·09	2·09	2·09	8·36
Water tanks (auxiliary)	2	8·00		8·00		16·00
Water in tanks -	—	76·50		76·50		153·00
					Total -	177·36

SUMMARY OF ALTERATIONS.

			Tons	cwts.	qrs.	lbs.	ozs.
Removed from after car - - -			2	10	1	18	5
Removed from engine - -			—	1	0	25	.5
Total removed -			2	11	2	16	4
Total replaced - - - - -			1	4	3	11	8¼
	lbs.	ozs.					
Less 2 after propeller thrust wires.	9	4½					
Less 1 auxiliary water tank on deck	9	5					
			—	—	—	18	9½
Total replaced -			1	4	2	20	14¾
Total removed - - - -			2	11	2	16	4
Total replaced - - - -			1	4	2	20	14¾
Weight reduced -			1	6	3	23	5¼

APPENDIX II.

CONTENTS OF SPECIFICATION

I.—Outline Description.
II.—Details of Hull and Materials.
III.—Details of Fixtures other than actual Hull
IV.—Details concerning the Outer Cover
V.—Details concerning the Gasbags.
VI.—Details concerning the Machinery.
VII.—Fittings and Instruments.
VIII.—List of Spares.
IX.—Tests and Trials.

I.—OUTLINE DESCRIPTION.

General Particulars of Design.

1. The airship is to be of the rigid type.
2. The net gas capacity is to be not less than 750,000 cubic feet.
3. The external dimensions of the ship are to be approximately as follows :—

	Feet.
Outside diameter of hull - - - - -	53
Overall length - - - - - - -	520
Maximum overall height - - - - -	72

4. The ship is to be fitted with four motors of 170 guaranteed brake horse-power each.
5. The ship is to attain a speed of at least 45 miles per hour for full power of the engines.
6. A minimum of 5 tons is to be available for disposable weights.

II.—DETAILS OF HULL AND MATERIALS.

7. The design of the rigid ariship, as shown on Drawing No. L—1B, is to be generally in conformity with the existing Zeppelin constructions.

8. In transverse section the hull is to be a uniform polygon of 17 sides. The overall outside diameter being 53 feet and the overall length 520 feet.

9. The shape of the hull and the cars is to be made in conformity with the best form practically for head resistance.

10. In the length of the hull there are to be 17 gasbags sections, the length of each at the parallel portion of the hull being 30 feet.

11. At the places where the gasbags end there are to be transverse frames with transverse wire bracing, as shown in Drawing No. L—18B.

12. Where wires crossing each other are liable to chafe, they are to be suitably protected.

13. Radial wires to give the necessary fixity of shape are to be fitted, connecting the joints of the framing to a centre ring.

14. Suspension wires are to be fitted running from the top corners of the keel to the joints of the framing.

15. At the upper part of the frame cross wires are to be fitted to assist in taking the end pressure from a gasbag when the adjacent one is empty.

16. External wiring is to be fitted between the channel members of the longitudinal frames as shown on Drawings Nos. L—3B, L—18B.

17. Between the points on the longitudinal frames where the external wires cross, tubular struts are to be fitted as may be approved by the Admiralty.

18. In the panels of the framing in way of the cars are to be fitted special large diagonal wires from corner to corner of the panels, in addition to those mentioned in paragraph 16.

19. To take the lift of the gasbags, nets are to be fastened between the inner members of the longitudinal frames, and suitably adjusted. The nets to be stretched and tested to the satisfaction of the Admiralty before the erection in the ship.

20. The keel to be specially designed to be able to take all vertical forces and bending moments.

21. *Longitudinal Girders.*—The longitudinal girders are to be of a triangular section, comprising a channel member ·9 inch by ·9 inch by ·9 inch by ·05 inch at the apex, and two triangles, each ·9 inch by ·9 inch by ·05 inch at the base. The depth to be 8 inches and the base width 5·2 inches. These members are to be connected to form the frame by diagonal bracing pieces riveted on and of suitable section, as shown on Drawings Nos. L—4B and 5B.

22. *Transverse Girders.*—The main transverse girders are to be built of channels and angles of the same section as the longitudinals. The depth of the frame is to be 7·6 inches, and the base width 4·8 iches, the difference of depth being due to the angle at which it joins the longitudinal frames. The apex angle of the triangle in both sets of girder is to be 30 degrees.

23. *Joints of Frames.*—The method of making the frame joints is to be as shown on Drawings Nos. L—4B and L—5B.

24. The method of attaching the various transverse wires will be as shown in Drawing No. L—6B.

25. *Stiffening in Way of Propellers.*—Additional frame members and bracing are to be built in as required to give the necessary support to the propeller brackets.

Special diagonal wires are to be fitted in the adjacent frame panels.

27. Arrangements are to be provided for the support of the ship when inflated in the shed, by means of vertical lugs on the top of the ship, or by other suitable devices. When deflated the ship is to be capable of being supported from under the keel.

28. Suitable arrangements are to be provided for lacing the bags to the top middle line longitudinals for inflation purposes, so as to distribute the load evenly over the whole length of the girder.

29. All mooring attachments are to be capable of withstanding a working load of at least 10 tons.

30. *Keel.*—This is to be designed to serve as a strong girder running continuously towards both ends of the hull, and to which the suspension wires transmit the lift of the gasbags.

A suitable footway is to be provided at the foot of the keel.

31. *Materials and Tests.*—The framework of the hull and cars is to be of duralumin of the following specification :—

(*a*) The tensile strength to be not less than 25 tons per square inch.

(*b*) Elongation is to be not less than 18 per cent. in 2 inches.

(*c*) In heavy channels the tolerance is to be not more than half thickness when cut to length.

In light channels the tolerance is to be "0."

In sheet the tolerance (thickness) is to be not more than 5 per cent.

(*d*) Bending tests to be carried out as required to the satisfaction of the Admiralty.

32. The wiring is to be of special high tensile steel throughout, having a strength of not less than 75 tons per square inch (elongation being 8 per cent. in 2 inches when headed). Special attention is to be paid to the shape of heads, so as to ensure that the shape of the heads does not produce a section of maximum weakness in the vicinity of the head.

33. All holes are to be drilled unless written permission to the contrary is obtained from the Admiralty.

34. All riveting is to be hydraulic, screw-pressed, or as approved by the Admiralty.

35. During construction the contractors are not to allow any workman to walk or climb on any portion of the hull (which is not designed as a gangway) without being properly supported by independent staying.

36. No part of the framework is to be used to secure tackles, &c., for hoisting weights.

37. All the necessary arrangements for weighing and recording weights are to be made to the satisfaction of the Admiralty.

The weights are to be kept in such a form that the weight of any particular item of the hull or fittings can be traced in detail; they are to be recorded in groups, the items in each group to be settled with the overseers. On completion of the airship a return, showing the actual detailed weights worked into the ship or placed on board, should be forwarded for record purposes.

38. The entire metal structure is to be covered with one thin coat of good elastic varnish so as to efficiently protect the metal against corrosion.

III.—DETAILS OF FIXTURES OTHER THAN THE ACTUAL HULL.

39. *Cabin.*—A cabin is to be constructed at the middle of the keel. It is to be fitted with the necessary furnishings.

40. The following fittings are to be provided :—

A wireless telegraphy compartment of suitable dimensions for the reception of the apparatus, which will be provided by the Admiralty.

A division of the cabin into two portions, one for the officers and one for men.

Sleeping accommodation for 50 per cent. of the crew.

Cupboard for stowage of food and mess utensils.

Hanging hooks for clothes.

Suitable seating and messing accommodation.

Latrine (designed to also serve as a photographic dark-room).

41. *Gondolas.*—There are to be two gondolas, designed to carry effectively the motors and other loads, and to give convenient space for the crew and all the necessary fittings. The external form of the gondolas is to be such as to reduce head resistance to a practicable minimum. They are to be constructed of duralumin sections and covered with an external sheeting of duralumin plates, the whole being suitable for alighting on the water.

42.

43. Suitable covers are to be provided and fitted over the gondolas to provide protection for the occupants.

44. The vertical height between the gunwale of the gondolas and the lowest part of the gasbags is to be not less than 15 feet.

45. A space of at least 5 feet (vertically) open to the air is to be provided between the top of the cover and the bottom of the keel.

46. Suitable buffers are to be provided and fitted under the gondolas to diminish shock of landing.

47. A suitable chart table and cupboard are to be provided and fitted in the foremost gondola.

48. Steel boxes for the engine tools are to be provided.

49. Space is to be left in the after part of the foremost gondola for installing a capstan after acceptance of the ship, if desired.

50. Suitable arrangements for draining the gondolas are to be provided and fitted.

51. Arrangements are to be provided in the construction for the quick detachment of the gondolas from the hull of the ship.

52. In the foremost gondola a clear space of at least 10 feet by 6 feet is to be arranged for between the instrument table and the engine bulkhead for the use of the controlling officers.

53. Provision is to be made for mounting a 1-pr. gun in each gondola.

54. *Observation and Gun Platforms and Tubes.*—An observation platform is to be provided and fitted on the top of the ship.

55. A gun platform is to be provided and fitted on the top of the ship for mounting two Maxim guns.

56. The gun platform is to be at Frame No. 3, and the observation platform at Frame No. 8.

57. Access to these platforms is to be provided and fitted by two tubes of fabric stiffened with rings and fitted with suitable ladder rungs; space is to be provided at the top of the tube to gun platform for storing boxes of ammuntition, and arragnements for hoisting them up are to be provided.

58. *Walking-way.*—A suitable walking-way is to be provided and fitted on top of the ship to give communication between the observation station and gun platform, and also to provide access to the various valves.

59. *Fins and Steering Rudders.*—The vertical and horizontal fins are to be as shown on Drawings Nos. L 91, 92, and 93.

60. Arrangements are to be provided to facilitate water running off the fins.

61. The rudders are to be as shown on Drawings L 91 and 92.

62. One set of control wires to the rudders is to be fitted to each gondola and worked by a suitable handwheel. Each set is to be capable of being thrown out of gear when the other is in use.

63. *Auxiliary Steering Rudders.*—Auxiliary steering rudders of the same general design as the main steering rudders are to be fitted where shown on Drawing No. L—1B. They are to be arranged to be controlled from the after gondola by a suitable handwheel and control wires.

64. *Horizontal Rudders, or Elevators and Gearing.*—The horizontal rudders are to be as shown on Drawings Nos. L 91 and 92. They are to be arranged to be controlled from the forward and after gondolas through suitable gearing. Each portion is to be capable of being thrown out of gear when the other is in use. Suitable handwheels are to be fitted.

65. All fins, rudders, and elevators are to be covered with material similar to that used on the bow sections.

66. The centres of pressure of the rudders and elevators are to be in rear of the turning axes.

67. Access to rudders, elevators, and bow cap when the ship is in flight is to be provided and fitted.

IV.—DETAILS CONCERNING THE OUTER COVER.

68. The outer cover is to be of unbleached linen fabric suitable to resist absorption and permeation of rain or moisture and to gain some insulation from external changes of temperature. It is to be provided with suitable means of attachment to the framing.

69. As far as possible the outer cover is to be made fire and water proof throughout; in wake of cars, central cabin, and gun platform this is essential. If considered necessary by the Admiralty, it is to be coated with a suitable varnish. The varnish or dope employed is to be such that it does not reduce the strength of the fabric by more than 10 per cent. (as measured before doping) in a weathering test of 100 days, unprotected from the direct action of the sun's rays. The varnish or dope must not disintegrate to form substances liable to damage either the outer cover or the frame to which it is attached, and necessary tests for these properties are to be carried out.

70. The outer cover is to be permeable to hydrogen, and to a certain extent permeable to air, except in wake of the gondola and forward of the gun platform.

71. Proper ventilating facilities are to be provided between the outer cover and the gasbags.

72. The upper half of the outer cover is to be coated with aluminium dust.

73. Each section of the airship is to have a separate sheet of outer cover; each sheet is to be capable of being removed or replaced at will. The fabric in each section is to be diagonally worked so as to serve as an additional shear bracing. Where each sheet of the outer cover meets, a suitable covering strip is to be provided and secured as approved.

74. The tensile strength of the outer cover is to be not less than 50 lbs. per inch run for a fabric weighing not more than 2·5 ozs. per square yard.

75. The bow sheets over the first and second bay spaces are to be of strength not less than 70 lbs. per inch run, and of weight not greater than 3½ ozs. per square yard.

76. The corners of the outer cover must be specially strengthened.

V.—DETAILS CONCERNING THE GASBAGS.

77. The ship is to be provided with 17 gasbags, the total volume of which is to be not less than 750,000 cubic feet.

78. The fabric is to be capable of standing a stress of at least 60 lbs. per inch run in warp and weft.

79. The permeability of the untreated fabric before skinning is to be not more than 25 litres per square metre per 24 hours.

80. The gasbags are to be lined with an inner skin of goldbeaters' skin in three thicknesses, and so treated as to eliminate formation of fungus.

81. Inspection glasses and fittings for taking the purity of the gas are to be supplied and fitted to each gasbag.

82. *Filling Connections.*—Filling connections are to be formed at the bottom of each gasbag, and so arranged as to be conveniently connected to outside filling pipes.

83. The filling pipes are to be provided with suitable means of sealing.

84. *Valves.*—A valve is to be fitted to the top of each gasbag adapted for hand control of the gas discharge, and also to open automatically at a pre-determined pressure.

85. A second valve is also to be fitted on the top of each gasbag for automatic release of excess of pressure only.

86. Provision is to be made so as to ensure that the discharge of the gas from the valves takes place direct to the atmosphere.

87. If constructed of a conducting material the valves and their seatings are to have permanent electrical connection between each other.

88. The effective area of the valves is to be sufficient to allow a rise of 1,000 feet per minute without dangerous increase of pressure, both valves being in operation at the same time.

89. Arrangements are to be made whereby the valves can be removed without deflating the gasbag.

90. Both valves are to be of a design whereby they are operated by variation of pressure at the bottom of the bag instead of at the top.

91. The valve cords are to be made of hemp.

92. No hydrogen is to be let into the gondolas in connection with the gasbag pressure gauges or for any other purposes.

93. Arrangements are to be considered for leading hydrogen exhaust discharge tubes aft of the gun-platform from all valves forward of this position.

94. Six suitable attachment points are to be fitted to each gasbag.

VI.—DETAILS CONCERNING THE MACHINERY.

95. *Engines.*—Four engines, each of 170 guaranteed b.h.p., are to be supplied and fitted, two in each gondola, to drive the propellers through suitable clutches, reversing gear, and tubular shafting.

96. Each motor is to drive its own propeller. Brakes are to be fitted to the propeller shafts to facilitate rapid stopping and reversing.

97. The radiators are to be fitted outside the gondolas, on each bow of the gondola, so that the minimum resistance is offered by them, and so that they may assist in warming the car.

98. The radiators are to be of a diagonal element type; they are to be interchangeable.

99. A regulation screen is to be fitted, if found necessary, to each radiator.

100. The exhaust pipes are to be water-cooled where they pass inside the gondola, and there must be no possibility, under any circumstances, of flame occurring in vicinity of exhaust outlet.

101. The temperature of the exhaust gases is to be not more than 300° Fahrenheit.

102. The petrol pump and its connections are to be entirely outside the crank case.

103. Efficient ventilation of the crank case is to be provided and fitted.

104. Efficient precautions against fires occurring in the carburettor, due to back fires, &c., are to be taken.

105. Arrangements are to be provided and fitted whereby each engine can be easily started by one man.

106. *Engine Bearers.*—The engines are to be carried on steel girders, which should be insulated from the framework of the ship to reduce vibration.

107. The capacity of the fuel tanks is to be sufficient to allow of at least 24 hours' running at full power.

(N.B.—This will be verified by the consumption results of the bench tests of the motors.)

108. The engines are to take their supply from a service tank carried in the keel above each gondola. The service tank is to be kept supplied by a pump driven off the engines, which takes the petrol from the main tanks.

109. An auxiliary hand pump is to be fitted to each service tank.

110. No petrol pipes are to be led over the engines or exhaust pipes unless efficiently screened to stop drip or leakage.

111. Provision is to be made for rapidly emptying petrol overboard by means of suitable valves of not less than 2½ inches diameter, when required in case of emergency.

112. A flexible pipe of at least 15 feet long to lead the petrol clear when being discharged is to be provided and fitted to each tank. This discharge fitting is to be adapted for use with a hand pump for filling the tanks.

113. A lighting set is to be installed to consist of the following :—

One dynamo set driven off either pairs of engines.
One emergency accumulator battery.
Navigation lights, lights in gondolas, cabins, &c.
One efficient searchlight.

114. Provision is to be made for driving the wireless telegraphy plant.

VII.—FITTINGS AND INSTRUMENTS.

115. *Ballast.*—The ship is to carry at least 2 tons of ballast.

116. Water ballast is to be carried in fabric bags suspended inside the keel and suitably distributed. The emptying of these bags is to be made by control from the forward car so that it can be done rapidly in case of emergency.

117. *Mooring Arrangements.*—All mooring arrangements are to be capable of standing a working load of at least 10 tons.

118. *Guys.*—Not less than 10 guys are to be fitted each side of the airship, of sufficient strength to hold the ship boardside on to a wind of 10 miles per hour with a factor of safety of 5.

119. All guys are to be of such a length, and so placed, that it is impossible for them to blow into the propellers.

120. The following mooring appliances are to be provided by the Contractor :—

Two handling ropes.
Short handling ropes every 30 feet (including those mentioned in clause 118).
One anchor rope forward.
One short wire on bow.

121. Voice pipes, telephones and telegraphs are to be provided as requisite between—

Forward and after gondolas.
Each gondola and central cabin.
Forward gondola and both platforms.

122. The following instruments are to be supplied and fitted in place by the Contractors :—

One aneroid, large dial, as made by Messrs. Short and Mason, in each gondola.
One aneroid, small.
One small recording barograph.
Two statascopes.
One maximum and minimum thermometer.
One Pitôt tube speed indicator.
Two clocks (eight-day type).
Two leak detectors.
Two longitudinal inclinometers.

Complete set of liquid pressure gauges (to each gasbag), graduated in British standard units.

Four revolution indicators with counters.

One "Tel" speed indicator and distance run recorder.

Engine-room telegraph (four speeds), two in each gondola, one to engines in same gondola, and one to engines in other gondola.

A gauge is to be fitted to each petrol tank, marked in pounds.

Four compasses are to be fitted—standard, steering (one in each gondola) and back-bearing; the steering and standard compasses are to be supplied and fitted by the Contractor, and are to be of approved Admiralty design; the back-bearing compass will be supplied by the Admiralty.

No magnetic substance is to be placed within 3 feet of the standard compass.

Two recording vertical acceleration indicators of a type to be indicated later, one fitted in each gondola.

All instruments are to be graduated in British standard units.

123. ***Fixture List.***—A fixture list is to be prepared and furnished by the Contractor, and, after verification by the overseers and officers concerned, the Contractor is to supply four fair copies, which are to be handed to the overseers as soon as possible after the acceptance of the ship.

IX.—TESTS AND TRIALS.

125. Before acceptance the ship or its component parts will be required to pass the following tests and trials :—

126. Portions of the gasbag fabric and outer cover material will be tested by the National Physical Laboratory, or as otherwise arranged by Admiralty, to ascertain whether it is up to the standard laid down above.

The gasbag fabric will be tested before and after skinning, and the permeability results obtained in each case are to be up to the present-day standards.

127. Portions of the material of the hull will be tested by the Admiralty inspectors, to ascertain whether it complies with the specified requirements.

128. The gondolas will be subjected to a practical test as to their watertightness and buoyancy, and to aid in this test, the complete car will be weighed.

129. *Valve Test.*—Valves are to blow off freely, at not more than 10 mm. of water pressure at bottom of bag. To be tight at 5 mm. This test will be repeated when all bags are fitted in ship.

130. The net lift of ship is to be as specified.

131. The disposable lift is to be not less than 5 tons with the gasbags 95 per cent. filled with hydrogen at a barometric pressure of 29·5 inches and temperature 55° Fahrenheit.

132. The disposable lift is to provide for carrying the crew, store and food, wireless installation, armament and explosives, fuel, lubricating oil and water ballast, instruments specified in clause 122, when the ship is trimmed at ground level.

133. This test will be carried out with the ship completely inflated, the necessary allowance for the 95 per cent. inflation and for barometric pressure and temperature being made by calculation. In addition, if desired, any of the disposable weights referred to above which may be on board will be removed for this test, and the actual lift measured by placing sand and other ballast of known weight in the ship. This sand or ballast

is to be supplied, weighed, placed on board, and removed by the Contractors, and at their expense and risk, and all necessary assistance to the Admiralty Officers conducting the test is to be given.

134. During this test the trim of the ship is to be horizontal with the ballast in its designed position.

135. *Leakage of Gas.*—Not to exceed 1 per cent. per diem. To be measured over a period of not less than seven days, commencing with all gasbags full, normal valve setting, due allowance being made for changes of barometric pressure and of temperature during the test.

ENGINE TRIALS.

136. *On the Bench.*—(*a*) A 24 hours' bench trial of one engine as a complete unit, to be run in two trials of 12 hours' duration each. No readjustments, cleaning, or other work being done on the engine during the interval between the two trials. During these trials, temperatures, consumption of fuel, oil and cooling water, maximum and mean h.p., &c., to be measured.

A minimum of 95 per cent. of the specified horse-power is to be obtained.

During the trials the cooling water discharged is to be not less than 200° Fahrenheit.

The remaining three engines will be run for six hours each under similar conditions.

(*b*) After these trials the engines to be dismounted as required by the Inspecting Officer, examined, re-erected, and run for two hours continuously at full power.

(*c*) Stopping, starting, and controllability tests will be carried out.

(*d*) When finally erected in the ship the entire plant to be tested for controllability, reversibility, and general efficiency, while actually driving the propellers, &c. This trial will be of two hours' duration, during which the ship must be completely air-borne for at least one hour. This trial to be carried out before the ship leaves the shed.

(*e*) The engines must be capable of running for at least a quarter of an hour inclined at an angle of 25° up and down in a fore and an aft direction, and at an angle of heel of 10° degrees either way; this will be tested practically, and the Contractors are to provide and fit the necessary appliances to permit of these tests being carried out on the bench.

(*f*) The supply of petrol to the engines must be constant and independent of the inclinations of the ship up to the above limits.

PROPELLERS.

137. Propellers to be tsted for efficiency on the whirling table. Static thrust to be measured. Maximum speed to be equivalent to an engine speed of 1,200 revolutions per minute. The efficiency is to be not less than 70 per cent. at a forward speed of 45 miles per hour and a rate of revolution corresponding to normal running at specified power. Each propeller will be run for half an hour at an overload equivalent to a 15 per cent. increase of speed above the normal running of the engine at its specified power.

PETROL DISCHARGE.

138. The petrol must be capable of being discharged overboard (without any possibility of ignition, danger from the exhaust pipe or silencers of exhaust gases) at a rate of 100 gallons a minute from all tanks. Discharge when not in use to be perfectly petrol-tight.

139. All petrol tanks are to be tested to an internal pressure of 10 lbs. per square inch.

140. All fittings and pipes are to be tested to 45 lbs. per square inch when complete for service.

141. Dynamos, lighting plant, wireless alternator or any auxiliary machinery fitted must carry out a trial, performing adequately the duty for which they are intended for not less than two hours.

142. The ship will be required to complete a two-hours' flight under the conditions specified below :—

(*a*) To fly at full specified power for at least 30 minutes.

(*b*) To develop a minimum speed of 45 miles per hour when engines are working at full specified power.

(*c*) To rise a minimum height of 2,000 feet during the flight and to remain there for at least 30 minutes.

(*d*) To satisfy the Admiralty representatives that she is satisfactory as regards stability, steering, and turning circles.

(*e*) The rudders and elevators must be easily workable by one man.

(*f*) The communications, voice-pipes, telegraphs and illuminations are to be proved efficient with the engines running at full power.

If the two-hours' flight is not satisfactory, a further flight may be required.